KALEIDOSTARS

TOBY LISCHKO

AQS Publishing

The American Quilter's Society or AQS is dedicated to quilting excellence. AQS promotes the triumphs of today's quilter, while remaining dedicated to the quilting tradition. AQS believes in the promotion of this art and craft through AQS Publishing and AQS QuiltWeek®.

CONTENT EDITOR: CAITLIN M. TETREV
ILLUSTRATIONS: TOBY LISCHKO
GRAPHIC DESIGN: ELAINE WILSON
COVER DESIGN: MICHAEL BUCKINGHAM/SARAH BOZONE
QUILT PHOTOGRAPHY: CHARLES R. LYNCH
HOW-TO PHOTOGRAPHY: TOBY LISCHKO
ASSISTANT EDITOR: ADRIANA FITCH
DIRECTOR OF PUBLICATIONS: KIMBERLY HOLLAND TETREV

Additional copies of this book may be ordered from the American Quilter's Society, PO Box 3290, Paducah, KY 42002-3290, or online at www.ShopAQS.com.

Attention Photocopying Service: Please note the following—Publisher and author give permission to print pages 87–92.

American Quilter's Society
www.AmericanQuilter.com

LIBRARY OF CONGRESS CATALOGING-IN-PUBLICATION DATA

PENDING

-- ◆ -- DEDICATION -- ◆ --

As I travel and teach I have found that quilters are alike all over the country. They make me feel I belong to the guild I am speaking to and I leave knowing that I have made new quilting friends. I have to thank the many hosts (and their husbands) who have opened up their home and hearts to me while I am on the road and the students in my workshops, who never fail to compliment me on my teaching abilities. I have never met a quilter I didn't like and who wasn't willing to go out of their way to make me feel welcome! This book is dedicated to all of them.

COVER QUILT: MARDI GRAS, detail. Full quilt on p. 54.

TITLE PAGE: FUN HOUSE MIRRORS, detail. Full quilt on p. 42.

LEFT: ROYAL GARDEN, detail. Full quilt on p. 48.

-- ACKNOWLEDGMENTS --

There are many people who have helped me along my quilting journey. First and foremost, my husband of 43 years, Mike, a Marine Corps, Vietnam Veteran (a title he is very proud of). He has supported all of my ventures throughout the years we have been married. Even when it created some difficult times, he has never stopped me from pursuing my dreams.

I want to thank my parents who have always taught me to be the best at anything I put my mind to. Rosemary, my closest friend and traveling companion, who helps me with my workshops and always cheers me up when I am down. To Dolores who has been like a second mother to me and never fails to tell me how proud she is of me. My close friend Terri, who always fits time in to quilt my quilts when I'm at a deadline. Gloria and Lynn, who helped put the binding on my quilts at the last minute, and Marty, who helps me out in my shop and tries to keep me organized.

Thanks goes to the national teachers who have helped me along the way: Jackie Robinson, who taught me to quilt; Marty Michell, whose templates have inspired me to create my own; Sharyn Craig, whose basic sewing techniques I have built on, use daily, and pass on to my students; and Paula Nadelstern, who designs such fun fabrics to play with. In the last two years, she has personally asked me to work with her fabrics and uses my samples in her workshops. I am honored to work with her and love to hear it when she tells me I "get it" when working with her fabrics. There is no better honor, than to hear from other accomplished quilters about how much they like your work.

I am especially thankful for the many magazine editors who put me in print and made me feel good about my work. The fabric companies who have come to me to create quilts with their wonderful fabric collections and given me fabrics for this book including: RJR, Benartex, In The Beginning, and Timeless Treasures. Last but not least, I want to thank the American Quilter's Society for choosing to print this book, Kimberly who saw great potential in me and my quilts, and my talented publication team for putting it all together.

RIGHT: MARDI GRAS, detail. Full quilt on p. 54.

-- CONTENTS --

BURGUNDY AND LACE, 36" x 36", made and quilted by the author.

KALEIDOSTARS ✳ Toby Lischko

-- INTRODUCTION --

I have always been fascinated with stars both complex and simple. I am drawn to designers like Paula Nadelstern and Jinny Beyer, who create such intricate designs by selectively cutting fabrics and making wonderful kaleidoscope designs. When I can put the two together I find the results to be amazing. It can help a blah block become an amazing block. Take a plain block and turn it into a spectacular block. It gives life to a quilt that needs some pizzazz! It can make your quilt stand out among others.

This block came about after I designed BURGUNDY AND LACE for Paula Nadelstern with one of her new collections.

I started with a traditional Kaleidoscope block (fig. 1).

I wanted some diamonds in the block so I added some lines (fig. 2).

This is the block I used for her quilt (fig. 3).

After I had made that quilt, I wanted to come up with a similar design but with eight (8) diamonds instead of four (4) so I added more lines (fig. 4).

Thus the Kaleidostar block was born! Then I started playing with Paula Nadelstern fabrics and discovered that playing with just symmetrical fabrics, I could create a wide variety of looks. I could use one (1) fabric to create many different looks. Two (2) fabrics mixed together would result in a very different appearance, and three (3) fabrics really made the quilt pop!

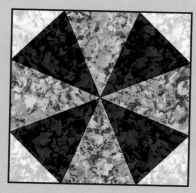

Fig. 1

Fig. 2

Fig. 3

Fig. 4

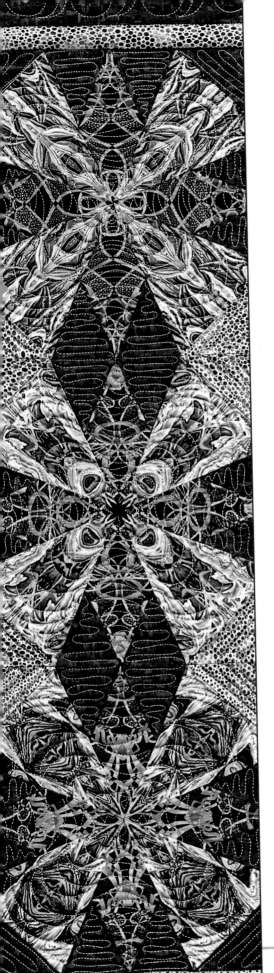

INTRODUCTION

I wanted to write this book to show off many of the wonderful design possibilities with this block using mainly symmetrical fabrics. I used Electric Quilt 7© to import the fabrics and manipulate them so that I could see what it would look like before I began to sew. I could also play with fabric placement and layouts to see which looked best.

One of the great things about this block is that it has no "y" seams. Not that they are difficult, but I know some quilters avoid blocks that have "y" seams because they think they are too difficult. This block is pieced in sections, which makes it easy to piece and comes in two (2) different finished sizes, 13" and 17".

I wrote this book for all of those quilters who want to take their quilting to the next level and put some variety into their projects. I have provided step-by-step directions and broken them down, so that anyone can be successful at it. There are templates at the back of the book and instructions for making your own templates, but also how you can order the acrylic templates for better accuracy.

I want you to be inspired after reading this book and playing with this block. My basic philosophy is, "Quilting should be fun!" I want you to enjoy the process. The quilt patterns in the following pages are for inspiration and layout possibilities. Your quilts will not look exactly the same because your fabric choices may create a completely different look. The symmetrical fabrics you choose will make all of these quilts, not just replicas of my quilts, but will be unique to your taste in design and colors. You will be proud that you have made something that was of your own creation. So have fun with this book, create your own blocks, and make quilts that you love to keep or give away and to really impress your friends and family. You should always enjoy what you make and have fun sharing it and inspiring others. I certainly have.

LEFT: BURGUNDY AND LACE, detail. Full quilt on p. 6.

Where Should You Begin?

I recommend that you read through "Getting Started" on pp. 11–21 and "Constructing the Kaleidostar Block" on pp. 22–27 before beginning to make the quilts. You need to understand what symmetrical fabrics look like and how you can find designs to work with. Fabric choices are discussed in great details, describing how you get different looks by manipulating the diamonds. You will learn how to work with mirrors to see the myriad of patterns and designs that are created when the center of the block comes together. Mirrors are not required to find the designs but used as an aid for designing. These chapters also show you how to use the templates and how to selectively cut for perfect repeats every time you cut them out. I included the tools I like to work with for more accurate cutting and piecing.

Getting Started, beginning on p. 11, introduces you to different types of symmetrical fabrics, plus how to put colors together for the best effect or to create the effect you want. It also demonstrates how to make and use your own templates. I discuss the quilting tools that I personally use for better cutting and piecing, along with how to use mirrors to find repeats. I demonstrate how to cut out the eight (8) repeats, so that they are perfect replicas of each other, and to help you create your own designs.

Constructing the Kaleidostar Block, beginning on p. 22, gives you step-by-step directions and piecing tips on how to construct the block. You will need to refer back to this chapter for each of the quilts. I suggest that

you make a couple of "test" blocks with scraps, before making the quilts in this book. Practice makes perfect and you will find the block gets easier the more you piece it. I illustrate how I get a perfect ¼" seam every time, which is *extremely* important for the block to be accurate. There are many seams in this block and for every seam that is not accurate, it affects the squareness of the block. I will also give you tips on how to check if you are piecing accurately as you sew, pressing tips, and how to correct a block that is not quite "perfect." Of course I don't expect everyone to make "perfect" blocks. Even all of my blocks are not "perfect," they just look like they are. The most important point I'm trying to make is that you need to be "consistent" with your seam allowances. Consistency helps the seams come together. I want you to realize that this block is *doable* and you should not be intimidated by the look of it.

The Quilts, beginning on p. 29, contains the eight (8) quilt patterns. They are divided into three (3) different categories. They all involve selective cutting and manipulation of the fabric in the diamond, using one (1) or more fabrics, to create different effects in the center. Each individual pattern will describe the process in more detail and include fabric suggestions. It will also indicate which size block is used to make the quilt, either 13" or 17".

The first category of quilts, are made with one symmetrical fabric. The first quilt, PARFAIT, p. 30, has all of the repeats cut from the same design and every other diamond is rotated. This would be a good first quilt to make. There are only four (4) 17" blocks in this quilt, and since the diamonds are rotated, you do not have to match any of the fabric repeats. ELECTRIFYING, p. 35, uses the same fabric but has two different cuts from the same fabric. ROYAL GARDEN, p. 48, has all of the repeats cut from the same area of the fabric and all of the diamonds are going in the same direction. This is a difficult quilt to start with, because there is precision piecing to get all of the fabric pattern edges to match. FUN HOUSE MIRRORS, p. 42, uses a symmetrical fabric and is cut to create a mirrored effect, meaning that where the two (2) diamonds come together they create the mirror image. This is also a difficult one to start with because the edges of the designs all also have to match.

The second category of quilts combines two (2) different fabrics. MARDI GRAS, p. 54, has two different symmetrical fabrics in coordinating colors. They are alternated in the center of the block. CARIBBEAN BLUE, p. 59, has two (2) different fabrics, one that is symmetrical and one is not, that coordinate with each other. CARNIVAL, p. 64, has two (2) fabrics that are the same overall design, but one has a light background and one has a dark background. The diamonds are cut from the same motif on both fabrics and are sewn together so that the design from the light one blends into the same design from the dark one. This is another difficult quilt to piece due to all of the precision matching that has to be done.

The third category of quilt uses three (3) different symmetrical fabrics used in different blocks and in a variety of settings. This is seen in the final quilt NORTHERN LIGHTS, p. 68.

Finishing Techniques, beginning on p. 73, has basic quilt assembly for straight and on-point settings, directions on construction of borders, including mitered borders and bindings, and options for piecing backs.

The Quilt Gallery, beginning on p. 81, is a gallery of quilts from workshops that I have taught over the last year. Each of the students' quilts has their own unique "signature." I derived a lot of pleasure knowing that they "wanted" to finish the quilts, because they had fun playing with the fabrics. They felt that because they were involved in the creative process by looking for designs for the star, they had created their own version and did not just make a copy of mine.

The Templates, beginning on p. 86, contains the templates you will need to make before starting on the quilts.

I've tried to include enough different kinds of quilts in this book so that anyone can find something that piques their interest. They range from simple four-block patterns to small and large wall quilts with straight and on-point settings. If you just enjoy looking at beautiful quilts, then you will definitely enjoy reading this book. I certainly had fun making them!

GETTING STARTED

Choosing Fabrics

How many times have you gone to a quilt shop, found a beautiful symmetrical fabric, and asked yourself "What could I do with this?" You are stumped so you don't purchase it. This book will attempt to show you many different ways that you can use those fabrics.

This is my favorite part of the design process. Once you start using mirrors to create different effects with blocks, you will never look at fabric in the same way. Whenever I walk into a quilt shop, I can't resist purchasing fabric that I know will make fantastic star blocks.

These are a few basic things that I look for when making the Kaleidostar block.

What Are Symmetrical Fabrics?

If you can draw an imaginary line down the middle of a design on the fabric and it is divided into identical halves, it is symmetrical. There are many different types of symmetrical fabrics. There is the print that just goes in one direction, horizontal or vertical only, as in this image from the Timeless Treasures Eden collection by Chong-a Hwang (fig. 1–1).

Fig. 1–1

It is easy to see the symmetrical line. This particular fabric pattern repeats the same design along both symmetrical lines, just offset by half of the design.

Fig. 1–2

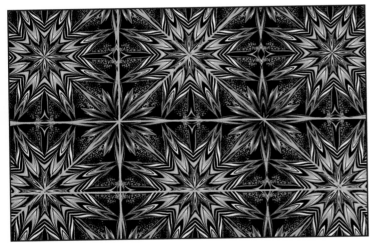

Fig. 1–3

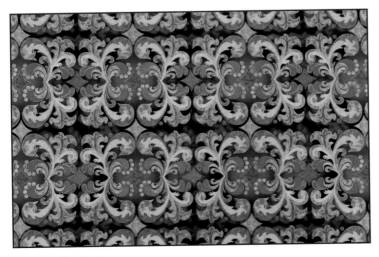

Fig. 1–4

Sometimes the fabric has symmetry in two (2) directions, horizontal and vertical as in this fabric collection called Fabracadabra by Paula Nadelstern with Benartex (fig. 1–2).

It can also go three (3) directions: horizontal, vertical, and diagonally as in this one by Paula Nadelstern (fig. 1–3).

No matter which one you pick they all can be used in similar ways. Some just have more choices in how many different kinds of patterns you can find.

What Else Should You Look For?

High Contrast and Lots of Colors

I usually like to work with fabrics that have a high contrast between the background and the pattern. It brings out the design better in the center of the star. In addition, if there are many different colors in the design, it gives me more choices to pick from for the patches surrounding the star. This fabric is a good example because it has a bright background plus a large variety of colors to choose (fig. 1–4). This fabric is used in the PARFAIT quilt, p. 30.

In some fabrics it can be difficult to see the symmetry and you don't notice them until you start to play with them. These fabrics are usually very busy, but can create very unique designs. Paula Nadelstern's fabric Tangles, from her newest collection, Fabracadabra is one of those. I really had to play with it to find interesting designs. All of the colors tend to blend together, making it a challenge to show off the repeat. Placing it with a second fabric helps bring out the design. (fig. 1–5). I used this fabric in MARDI GRAS, p. 54. This is what it looks like in the block (fig. 1–6).

Fig. 1–5

FABRIC COLLECTIONS

I also like fabric collections, because many times there are multiple color ways of the same pattern. These two (2) fabrics, called Carnival, by Jinny Beyer with RJR Fabrics, are good examples and are used in my CARNIVAL quilt, p. 65. Having dark and light backgrounds make a good contrast when alternating patches in the center of the block (figs. 1–7, 1–8, and 1–9).

Fig. 1–6

Fig. 1–7

Fig. 1–8

Fig. 1–9

Fig. 1–10

Fig. 1–11

These fabrics, called Paradise by Jason Yentor of In The Beginning Fabrics, are another good example of coordinating prints in different color ways (figs. 1–10 and 1–11).

Coordinating Fabrics

For the surrounding part of the center star, you have to determine what kind of effect you want to create. I have used a variety of fabric placements around the star in each of the quilts. I do tend to use tone-on-tones because I do not want those fabrics to take the focus off of the kaleidoscope design I am trying to create. By changing the fabric placement, it creates different effects with the connecting blocks. As you look through the quilts in this book, you will see how those fabrics interplay with each other. Of course there are no rules for fabric placement in this block. It is fun to experiment and try different settings and colorings.

These are good tone-on-tones to use with symmetrical fabrics (figs. 1–12a through 12h).

Fig. 1–12a

Fig. 1–12b

Fig. 1–12c

Fig. 1–12d

Fig. 1–12e

Fig. 1–12f

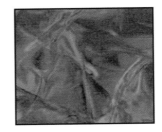

Fig. 1–12g

Fig. 1–12h

Quilting Tools

There are some basic tools that I always use when getting ready to make the Kaleidostar block (fig. 1–13).

Templates – Heavy clear template plastic is preferable if you make your own. Purchased acrylic templates are available in a 13" and 17" set on my website www.gatewayquiltsnstuff.com, (fig. 1–14) or you can ask your local quilt shop to carry them.

Adhesive tape for using on the back of the templates.

Fig. 1–13. PHOTO: CHARLES R. LYNCH

Small rotary cutter, 18mm is best, especially when fussy-cutting, so you do not cut into other designs you might want to use. The 18mm is good too. Template sizes any larger than those make them difficult to control when cutting around the template.

Any type of foam padding (I find it in the foot department) for establishing an exact ¼".

A seam gauge with ¼" reference holes.

Silk pins, .5 mm or smaller. Don't be fooled by a package that states "silk pins." Be sure to look at the width of the pin. I like pins that are .4 mm.

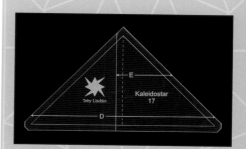

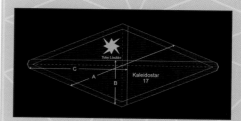

Fig. 1–14. My acrylic templates
PHOTOS: CHARLES R. LYNCH

Fig. 1–15. PHOTO: CHARLES R. LYNCH

Threads should be a "fine" weight. A 50-weight thread is good. You can use either a good long Egyptian cotton or a polyester thread (fig. 1–15). Do not use cheap threads. They are very hard on your sewing machine and create a lot of lint build up in the bobbin area.

A set of mirrors – You can make your own by taping two same size mirrors together with duct tape or you can purchase them. I use Marti Michell's 6" square Magic Mirrors.

How to Use the Mirrors

To set the mirrors at the angle needed for the center, place the diamond template inside and lay a piece of tape across the top to set it. This will set the mirrors at a 45° angle so you will see eight (8) repeats when you look in the mirrors (fig. 1–16).

With a symmetrical fabric, what you see in the mirror is what you will get when you cut out the eight (8) repeats. These are some of the repeats that you can see when I move the mirrors down the center of the floral pattern on the Eden fabric used in the ROYAL GARDEN quilt, p. 48, (figs. 1–17a and 1–17b).

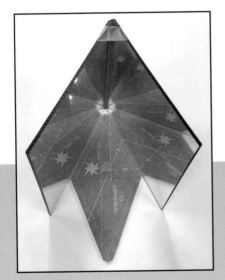

Fig. 1–16

Fig. 1–17a

Fig. 1–17b

Fig. 1–18a

Fig. 1–18b

Fig. 1–19

If you place the mirror on either side of the center line, as on this fabric, you will see a left and right image (mirror image) (figs. 1–18a and 1–18b). This is the effect I wanted to create with the FUN HOUSE MIRRORS quilt, p. 42 (fig. 1–19).

How Much Fabric Do I Need?

When purchasing fabric for each one of these projects you will need to take a variety of factors into account.

Scale

I have to admit, I don't always think about scale when I purchase fabrics to fussy-cut, I just buy it because I like it. I do have to think about it when I decide which project I want to use it in.

For both of the blocks you will want to avoid small prints because the effect you want to create gets lost in the center. For the 13" block you can use a medium or medium large print; however, for the 17" you should use medium large to a large print. Your best bet is, when you are shopping for fabrics, to take the templates with you so you can see how much of the designs will be within the seam allowances of both size templates. If the motif takes up the whole space and there is no "empty" space or background, you lose the repetition effect.

How About the Number of Repeats?

You have to look at the fabric to see how close together the repeats run across the selvage grain (length) and the width of the fabric. With symmetrical prints it is easier to find how many different repeats you can get when you are following along the symmetrical line. You do have to watch out for fabrics that have the repeats very far apart. It just means you have to purchase more yardage! It is hard to determine the yardage I will need on a project since every fabric is different

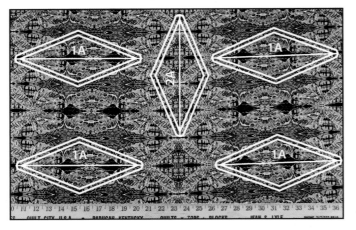

Fig. 1–20

Fig. 1–21. ELECTRIFYING, block detail. Full quilt on p. 35.

Fig. 1–22. PARFAIT, block detail. Full quilt on p. 30.

when I am fussy-cutting. The yardages given for the symmetrical fabrics in each of the patterns are estimates, because your fabrics may have different distances between repeats than the one I used in the quilt sample. It is best to get a little more, perhaps ½ to 1 yard more just to be safe. I have run out of fabric on some of my projects and have had to either change my original design or frantically look for more!

Since this block has eight (8) repeats in it, figure out how many repeats you can get from one yard of fabric and go from there (fig. 1–20). Many times when I find a fabric I like and I'm not sure what project I will be using it in, I may purchase twice the yardage I think I will need.

I do suggest that if you have never done any fussy-cutting before, that you start with a design that does not have to match on the sides of the center patches. Symmetrical designs require more matching and more accurate piecing in the center. Choose one of the patterns in this book that use the same fabric with two different cuts from it as in ELECTRIFYING (fig. 1–21) or cut from the same design where every other diamond is rotated as in the PARFAIT quilt (fig. 1–22). You will not have to worry about matching pattern lines when sewing either of these quilts.

Using the Templates

I find the easiest way to make the templates, if you have not purchased them, is by copying the template page on a copier (be sure there is no scaling when copying). Cut out the pieces from the paper (you do not have to be completely accurate at this time), tape the paper template to the back of the template plastic (roll a couple pieces of tape and place them on the top of the paper) and then cut them both out on the line. You will find this process much easier than trying to trace the template. It is very important to be as accurate as you can be, because the accuracy of your templates will give you the best results when piecing the block. Before you take off the paper, trace all of the lines and letters with a permanent marker. (The reason for placing the paper face up on the back of template plastic.) Take off the paper and label your templates with the letter, size, and name of the block it creates. Keep your templates in a ziplock bag to keep the sets together.

Now you get to play! First play with the mirrors to see how many kinds of different designs you can create by dragging the mirrors down the center of the symmetrical line. Each fraction of an inch will create a different pattern. After you find the design you want to cut out, place a couple pieces of rolled up tape on the back of the template and cut out your first piece. If I'm using template plastic, I like to use the 18mm rotary cutter. It will not cut into areas that I may want to use in another repeat, plus I have better control of it, keeping it from cutting into my template. If I am using purchased acrylic templates, the 18 mm or 28 mm rotary cutter works as well. If you use the larger rotary cutters, you have less control.

Once I find a design I like I will place the template on the fabric and line up the center line of the template to the center of the symmetrical line on the fabric. Carefully cut it out (figs. 1–22a, 1–22b, and 1–22c).

Fig. 1–22a   **Fig. 1–22b**   **Fig. 1–22c**

Now Here Is the Trick for Getting Perfect Repeats

Leave that fabric on the template because you will use it to find the next seven (7) (or whatever number you need) repeats. Simply find the area of the repeat. Place the template, with the fabric on it, onto the same repeat down or across from the first one, until it disappears into the fabric. All of the edges of the fabric on the template will connect to the same edges on the fabric underneath (fig. 1–23, p. 20). Cut it out and continue with this process until you have all of the repeats needed for each block.

Fig. 1–23

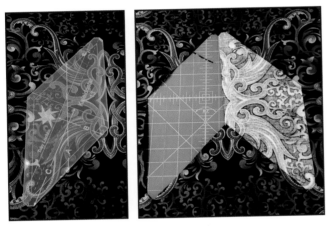

Fig. 1–24a   **Fig. 1–24b**

Fig. 1–24c. Fun House Mirrors, block detail. Full quilt on p. 42.

To create the mirror effect as in the Fun House Mirrors quilt, p. 42, you will cut out the first four repeats using the original cut patch Leave the original fabric patch on the template. Put the tape on the top side of the template, turn the template over and match the fabric edges again. This time you will be looking at the back of the fabric to match the edges. You can then take off the first cut and use the reverse cut as a reference to cut out the remaining three (3) reverse images. You will end up with four (4) left and four (4) right repeats (figs. 1–24a and 1–24b).

In the cutting instructions for the coordinating fabrics, I purposely have you cut the strips slightly larger than the template, see p. 21. This way if the edges are not perfectly aligned you have a little extra room to center the template to be sure that the top and bottom fabrics completely cover it. Be sure to trim off the corners to make piecing easier. The templates purposely have the corners trimmed so that when sewing the patches together there is no guess work as to how much you have to overlap the edges. They fit right on top of each other. Pay attention to grain line only on the coordinating fabrics. Since the center diamonds are cut on many different angles, you need to sew pieces around them that stabilize the block. I do not cut more than two layers at a time. The more layers you cut the more you reduce the accuracy of your cutting.

Now you are ready for the next chapter: Kaleidostar block construction.

Template Placement Cutting Guides

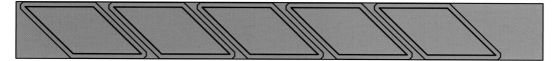

Template A Placement if not fussy-cutting

Template B Placement

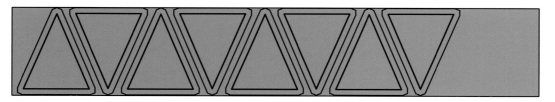

Template C Placement

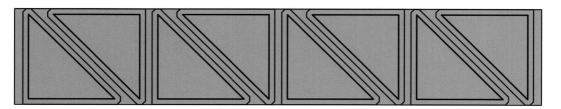

Template D Placement

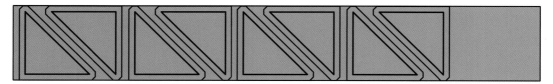

Template E Placement

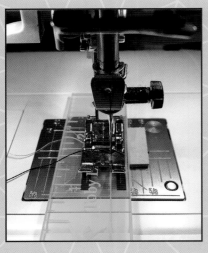

Fig. 2–1. Sewing machine seam guide PHOTO: CHARLES R. LYNCH

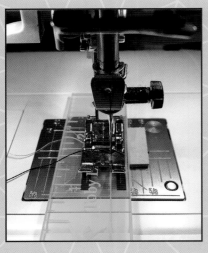

Fig. 2–2

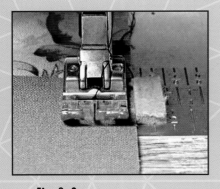

Fig. 2–3

CONSTRUCTING THE KALEIDOSTAR BLOCK

Piecing Tips

The number one priority of any piecing is an accurate ¼" seam allowance. I can't tell you how many times I have heard from quilters who have told me that when more than one person works on a quilt or does an "optional block" for a guild, none of the blocks are the same size. That is because everyone's definition of a "scant" quarter inch is different. It has been described as a thread's width or a "smidge" smaller. My theory is that if everyone does an accurate ¼" all of their blocks will be the same size. My method for creating an accurate ¼" is to use a special seam gauge that has a hole at the quarter inch (fig. 2–1). (Make sure it isn't a "scant" ¼" seam gauge.) Put the needle in the farthest right position as possible on your machine with the Number 1 or A Foot. The reason I do this is because some of the quilting feet do not cover both feed dogs and the result is that the fabric does not feed evenly under the foot. I struggled for years trying to create consistent seams using the edge of the quilting foot. I just couldn't see where the edge of the fabric was and it would move around under the foot.

After moving the needle to the right, place your needle in the ¼" hole of the seam gauge. Use a small strip of some type of raised padding that you can purchase at your local drug store in the foot department, and place it snug up against the edge of the gauge (fig. 2–2). I cut the padding ¼" wide with my rotary cutter and then into small ⅜" or ½" pieces.

You can see with my needle in this position, I can always see if my fabric is lined up with the ¼" guide (fig. 2–3).

There are four (4) things to consider when piecing any block. Cutting accurate patches, your ¼" seam, keeping the fabric edges together, and pressing not ironing.

The first thing I check, when my pieces are not fitting together, are the patches that I cut with the templates. There are times when the fabric on the bottom (or top) moves or the template slips slightly and you don't realize it. I will line them up with the template to see if they are cut too small or too big and either make an adjustment or cut out a new piece. My templates are created so that all of the edges align when you are ready to sew.

Consistency is the key. When you have a consistent ¼" seam from the top edge to the bottom edge, everything fits together better. Using the padding to the right of the presser foot, across from my needle and keeping the edges of the fabric touching it, I always have a consistent ¼" seam from the beginning to the end of my sewing edge. For any project I always check my

seams for accuracy. I use a "measure" as you go system when piecing. The best way to do this is, after you have completed the different sections of the blocks, place them on top of each other. Each of the sections should be exactly or pretty close to exactly the same size. By stacking them on top of each other, I can check to see if they are the same. It is easier to fix one or more as I go when I do this, than wait until the complete block is put together (fig. 2–4).

When there are numerous pieces in one block, every little fraction of an inch that is off affects the finished block. You have to always check to see if the edges of the two (2) fabrics are aligned. The bottom fabric has a tendency to move around and you may not notice it. You would be surprised to know that even if you are off ¹⁄₁₆" or ¹⁄₃₂" that it can throw off the entire block! With 28 pieces in this block, each fraction of an inch changes the block's alignment. Check your edges often and lift them up to check underneath as you sew, to make sure they are even. If one of your fabrics (usually

Fig. 2–4

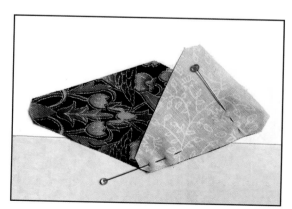

Fig. 2–5

the top one) has a tendency to "travel" and you end up with the top extending slightly beyond the bottom fabric at the end, simply place a pin at the end, holding the two (2) fabrics together. Because of the placement of the padding next to the foot, I do pin from the inside to the outside edge, with the point of the pin stopping at the edge. I will also occasionally "weave" the pin at the end to make sure the edges are secure before piecing (fig. 2–5, p. 23).

Pressing is the final step in making everything fit together when piecing. You can't always press seams to the dark fabrics and sometimes you even have to press them open. Since this block has eight (8) seams that come together in the center, the pressing instructions are very important in getting this block to lay flat in the center of the block (fig. 2–6). I have found that to make everything match in the center, it is better to press the seams open. That way they are not distorted at the center point. I also like to finger press all of my seams before I take them to the

iron. By doing this I can "feel" if the seams are pressed flat and I won't create a pleat when I press them with the iron.

Pay close attention to the order of piecing the patches together and the direction of pressing. Many of the beginning seams are pressed in such a way to have touching seams going in opposite directions around the block. To press the seams, I always use a dry iron. Steam tends to distort the block. For seams that are pressed to the side, I press from the top after finger pressing. For seams pressed open, I first press from the back then again from the front. When the entire block is complete, I will spray the block with water and then press from the back and top again, making sure all of the seams are pressed flat. The water also allows you to "block" the square in case it does not lay flat. If you have a slight "bump" in the center it means that your outside seams are slightly narrower than the inside seams. To fix this problem, spray it with water and press, radiating from the center and working towards the outside edge around the entire block.

Take your time when sewing. I always tell my students, "This is not a race." If you take your time, your accuracy increases and you will do less un-sewing! Also let the machine do the work for you. Many of the edges of the fabric are on the bias so do not push or pull your fabric as it is being sewn. It is okay to occasionally pull slightly on one of the patches in order to get the edges and corners to align correctly, as long as it is a very small difference.

Fig. 2–6. PHOTO: CHARLES R. LYNCH

General Piecing Instructions

Start out by laying out the complete block to the left of your sewing machine following this illustration (fig. 2–7). After each step, you will be referred back to this diagram. This block is constructed in eighths.

Fig. 2–7

Whole Block

1. Sew a Template C patch to the right side of the top of each Template A patch. Press in the direction of the arrows (fig. 2–8). You will have eight (8) total.

Fig. 2–8

> **Tip**
>
> If the edges of the seams are straight along the side then your seam allowance is correct. If not make an adjustment.

2. Sew a Template C patch to the left side of the top of each Template A patch. Press in the direction of the arrows (fig. 2–9).

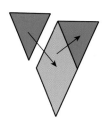

Fig. 2–9

3. Sew diamond sections together by pairs. Seams will be nested. Be sure to keep the same section on the right to keep your center design correct. Press seam open. Make four (4) quarter sections (fig. 2–10).

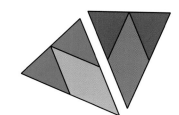

Fig. 2–10

> **Tip**
>
> Each section should be the same size. Place them on top of each other and check. If they are not, adjust your seam allowance.

4. Sew two (2) quarter sections together (fig. 2–11). Press seam open. Make two (2) halves.

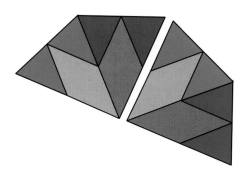

Fig. 2–11

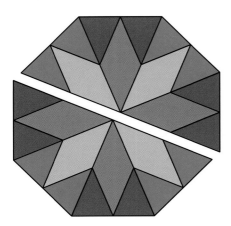

Fig. 2–12

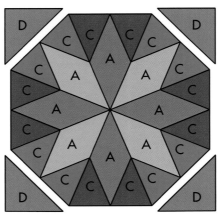

Fig. 2–13

5. Match center and seams, and sew halves together (fig. 2–12). Press center seams open.

6. Sew Template D patches to the corners (fig. 2–13). Press seams to D.

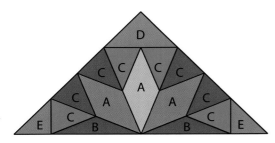

Fig. 2–14

Setting Triangles

For on-point settings (fig. 2–14).

7. Sew Template B patch to a Template C patch as illustrated (fig. 2–15). Press to B.

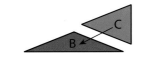

Fig. 2–15. Right Unit 5

8. Sew a Template E patch to the Right Unit 5 (fig. 2–16). Press to E.

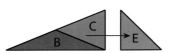

Fig. 2–16. Right Unit 6

9. Sew a Template B patch to a Template C patch as illustrated (fig. 2–17). Press to C.

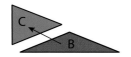

Fig. 2–17. Left Unit 5

10. Sew a Template E patch to a Left Unit 5 (fig. 2–18). Press to E.

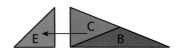

Fig. 2–18. Left Unit 6

11. Sew three (3) diamond sections following step 1 (fig. 2–19). Press seams open

12. Sew D to the corner (fig. 2–20). Press to D.

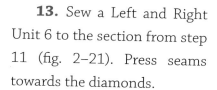

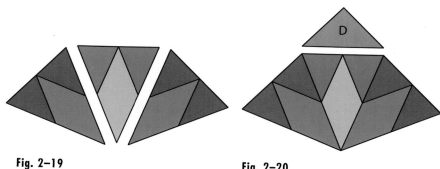

Fig. 2–19

Fig. 2–20

13. Sew a Left and Right Unit 6 to the section from step 11 (fig. 2–21). Press seams towards the diamonds.

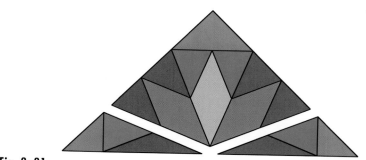

Fig. 2–21

Corner Block

For on-point setting (fig. 2–22).

14. Sew a diamond section as in step 1. Sew a Left and Right Unit 6 to it (fig. 2–23). Press seams towards the diamond.

See the templates on p. 86.

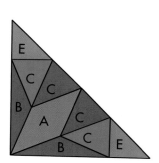

Fig. 2–22

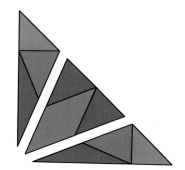

Fig. 2–23

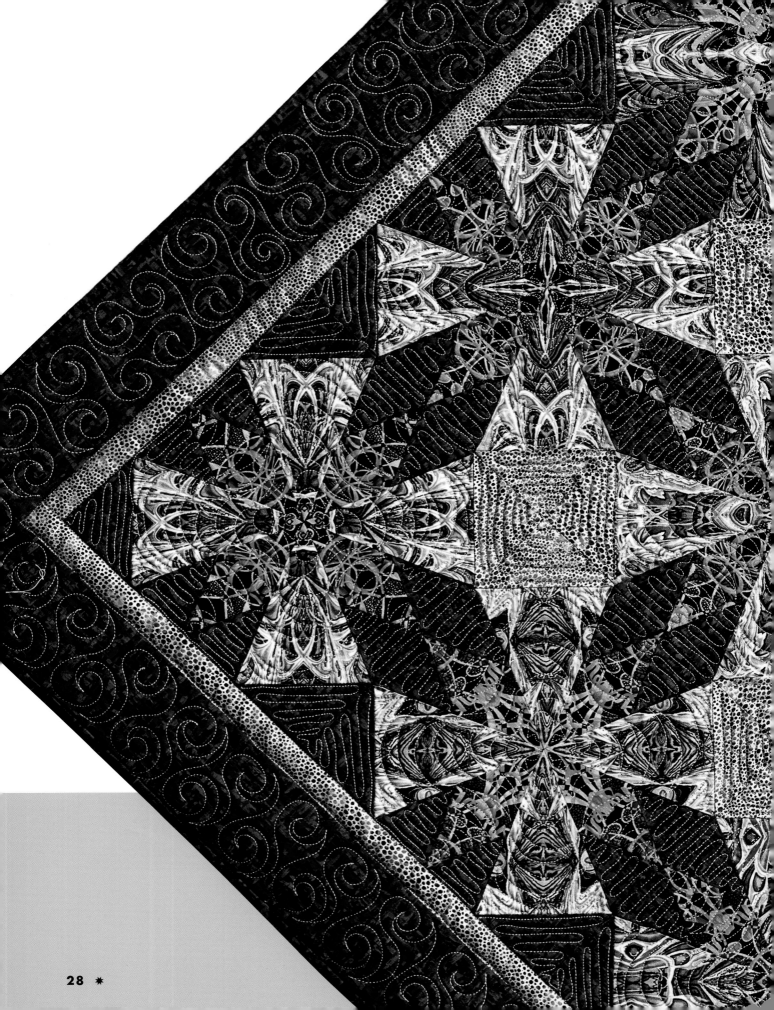

-◆- THE QUILTS -◆-

Using One Fabric

Using Two Fabrics

Using Three Fabrics

LEFT: BURGUNDY AND LACE, detail. Full quilt on p. 6.

Using One Fabric

Parfait, 47" x 47", made by the author.
Quilted by Sandy Etheridge, Affton, Missouri.

-- PARFAIT --

Quilt size: 47" x 47"
Block size: 17"

This quilt uses one (1) symmetrical print. The sections of the star blocks are cut from the same repeat. Every other diamond in the center is turned around. Choose a bright fabric with many colors so that you can pick four (4) coordinating tone-on-tones for the background. Then find a dark tone-on-tone for the frames around the blocks and corners. The border is divided to continue the colors from each of the blocks.

Fabric Requirements *(substitute your own colors)*

Fabric 1: Symmetrical fabric – 1 to 1½ yard
Fabric 2: Pink tone-on-tone – ¾ yard
Fabric 3: Blue tone-on-tone – ¾ yard
Fabric 4: Green tone-on-tone – ¾ yard
Fabric 5: Yellow tone-on-tone – ¾ yard
Fabric 6: Dark tone-on-tone – 1¼ yard
Backing: 3 yards
Batting: 52" x 52"

Cutting Instructions

(Based on 40" WOF-Width of Fabric)

Fabric 1

* Cut out four (4) different sets of eight (8) identical A repeats.

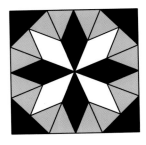

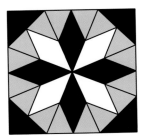

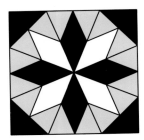

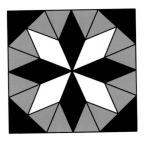

Fig. 3–1. Make 4 total blocks.

Fig. 3–2

Fabrics 2, 3, 4, and 5

* Cut one (1) 5" x WOF strip; subcut into sixteen (16) C of each color.
* Cut eight (8) 1½" x WOF strips; subcut into eight (8) 1½" x 17½" of each color and eight (8) 1½" x 19½" of each color.
* Cut one (1) 2½" x 21" of each color.
* Cut one (1) 2½" x 23" of each color.

Fabric 6

* Cut two (2) 5⅝" x WOF strip; subcut into sixteen (16) D.
* Cut two (2) 1½" x 39½".
* Cut two (2) 1½" x 41½".
* Cut five (5) 1½" x WOF strips.
* Cut six (6) 2¼" x WOF for binding.

Block Construction

1. Using the general piecing instructions, pp. 25–27, make one (1) of each color block following the illustrations (fig. 3–1). Each block uses the same color C and the same eight (8) repeats, rotated every other diamond.

Eight (8) Fabric 1 A, sixteen (16) Fabric 2 (or 3, 4, or 5) C, and Four (4) Fabric 6 D. Make one (1) of each color (4 total blocks).

2. Sew a 1½" x 17½" strip, matching the background fabric of the blocks, to the sides of each block (fig. 3–2). Press to strip.

3. Sew a 1½" x 19½" strip, matching the background fabric, to the top and bottom (fig. 3–3). Press to strip.

4. Sew a 1½" x 19½" Fabric 6 strip between 2 blocks (fig. 3–4). Repeat for other 2 blocks. Press to Fabric 6.

Fig. 3–3

Fig. 3–4

Quilt Construction

5. Connect the two (2) rows with the 1½" x 39½" Fabric 6 strip (fig. 3–5).

Border Construction

6. Sew a 1½" x 39½" Fabric 6 strip to each side. Press to Fabric 6. Sew a 1½" x 41½" Fabric 6 strip to the top and bottom (fig. 3–6). Press to 6.

7. Layout the four (4) blocks with the 2½" x 21" Fabric 2, 3, 4, and 5 strips on the sides and the 2½" x 23" on the top and bottom, matching the 2½" strips to the color of the blocks across from it (fig. 3–7, p. 34).

8. Sew the 2½" fabric sets together. Sew on sides first then top and bottom.

9. Sew the five (5) 1½" Fabric 6 strips short ends together. Trim to two (2) 1½" x 45½" and sew to sides (fig. 3–8, p. 34). Press to strip.

Fig. 3–5

Fig. 3–6

Fig. 3–7

10. Trim remaining strip to two (2) 1½" x 47½"**. Sew to top and bottom (fig. 3–9). Press to strip. (**You should measure the quilt to get your own personal measurement if it does not match the above.)*

11. Layer pieced backing, batting, and quilt top. Quilt as desired.

12. Follow the directions for sewing on the binding with the six (6) 2¼" Fabric 6 strips on pp. 79–80.

Fig. 3–8

Fig. 3–9

ELECTRIFYING!, 66¾" x 66¾", made and quilted by the author.

-- Electrifying! --

Quilt size: 66¾" x 66¾"
Block size: 17"

had bought this Paula Nadelstern fabric quite a few years ago and wasn't quite sure what I was going to do with it. As I was designing quilts for this book I noticed that there were two (2) different colors of the design, a gold/green combination and a pink/purple combination in the fabric. I decided to selectively cut the diamonds so that both colors would come together in the center. Pick one (1) fabric that has similar designs in different colors and selectively cut out two (2) different color ways.

I changed Template C patch by sewing two (2) strips together and then cutting them out, lining up the edge of the template along the bottom and top edge of the strip sets. This created the dark and light patches that alternate in the block. The pieced border continues the "electrical" feeling that the blocks give and the black and gold accents add to it. Because there is a pieced border, the accuracy of the piecing is important. Inside borders need to be cut to the size indicated.

Fabric Requirements *(substitute your own colors)*

Fabric 1: Symmetrical fabric – 2 to 2½ yards
Fabric 2: Silver (Light) – ⅓ yard
Fabric 3: Grey (Medium) – 1 yard
Fabric 4: Gold – 1¼ yard
Fabric 5: Black – 2⅞ yards for borders and binding
Backing: 4⅛ yards
Batting: 72" x 72"

Cutting Instructions

(Based on 40" WOF-Width of Fabric)

Fabric 1

* Cut out eighteen (18) different sets of four (4) identical A repeats. Divide into nine (9) set 1 and nine (9) set 2.

Fabric 2

* Cut five (5) 2½" x WOF strips.

Fabric 3

* Cut five (5) 2½" x WOF strips.
* Cut four (4) 4½" x WOF strips; subcut into sixty-four (64) 4½" x 2½" rectangles.
* Cut two (2) 2½" x 2½" squares.

Fabric 4

* Cut two (2) 5⅝" x WOF strips; subcut into sixteen (16) Template D.
* Cut five (5) 2½" x WOF strips.
* Cut four (4) 4½" x WOF strips; subcut into sixty-four (64) 4½" x 2½" rectangles.
* Cut two (2) 2½" x 2½" squares.

Fabric 5

* Cut one (1) 5⅝" x WOF strips; subcut into twelve (12) Template D.
* Cut sixteen (16) 2½" x WOF strips; subcut into (256) 2½" x 2½" squares.
* Cut six (6) 3" x WOF strips for border 1.
* Cut seven (7) 1½" x WOF strips for border 3.
* Cut seven (7) 2¼" x WOF strips for binding.

Block Construction

1. Sew a 2½" Fabric 2 strip to a 2½" Fabric 3 strip (fig. 4–1). Press to darker fabric. Make five (5) sets.

2. Lining up Template C along the bottom of the strip and rotating the template for every other cut, cut out seventy-two (72) with light on the bottom (C1) and seventy-two (72) with dark on the bottom (C2) (figs. 4–2a and 4–2b).

Fig. 4–1

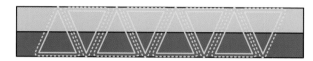

Fig. 4–2a

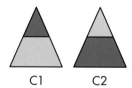

C1   C2

Fig. 4–2b

Block 1

1. Using the general piecing instructions, pp. 25–27, make four (4) blocks following the illustrations. Each block uses two (2) different sets of four (4) identical repeats, placed every other diamond.

Four (4) Fabric 1 A set 1, four (4) Fabric 1 A set 2, eight (8) pieced C1 templates, eight (8) pieced C2 templates, two (2) Fabric 4 D, and two (2) Fabric 5 D (fig. 4–3, p. 38).

Fig. 4–3. Block 1. Make 4.

Fig. 4–4. Block 2. Make 4.

Fig. 4–5. Block 3. Make 1.

Fig. 4–6

Fabric 3
Left unit

Fig. 4–7

Block 2

2. Using the general piecing instructions, pp. 25–27, make four (4) blocks following the illustrations. Each block uses two (2) different sets of four (4) identical repeats, placed every other diamond.

Four (4) Fabric 1 A set 1, four (4) Fabric 1 A set 2, eight (8) pieced C1 templates, eight (8) pieced C2 templates, and four (4) Fabric 4 D (fig. 4–4).

Block 3

3. Using the general piecing instructions, pp. 25–27, make one (1) block following the illustrations. This block uses two (2) different sets of four (4) identical repeats, placed every other diamond.

Four (4) Fabric 1 A set 1, four (4) Fabric 1 A set 2, eight (8) pieced C1 templates, eight (8) pieced C2 templates, and four (4) Fabric 5 D (fig. 4–5).

Pieced Border Section

4. Draw a diagonal line on the backs of the (256) 2½" Fabric 5 squares.

5. Place a 2½" Fabric 5 square on the right end of the 2½" x 4½" Fabric 3 rectangle as illustrated and sew along the drawn line (fig. 4–6). Trim seam to ¼" and press to Fabric 3.

6. Place a 2½" Fabric 5 square on the left end of the section from step 5 as illustrated and sew along drawn line. Trim seam and press to Fabric 3. Make twenty-eight (28) Fabric 3 Left units (fig. 4–7).

7. Repeat steps 5 and 6 with the 2½" Fabric 5 squares on the 2½" x 4½" Fabric 4 rectangles. Press to Fabric 5. Make twenty-eight (28) Fabric 4 Left units (fig. 4–8, p. 39).

8. Place a 2½" Fabric 5 square on the right end of the 2½" x 4½" Fabric 3 rectangle as illustrated and sew along drawn line (fig. 4–9). Trim seam to ¼" and press to Fabric 3.

9. Place a 2½" Fabric 5 square on the left end of the section from step 8 as illustrated and sew along the drawn line. Trim seam and press to Fabric 4. Make twenty-eight (28) Fabric 3 Right units (fig. 4–10).

10. Repeat steps 8 and 9 with the 2½" Fabric 5 squares on the 2½" x 4½" Fabric 4 rectangles. Press to Fabric 5. Make twenty-eight (28) Fabric 4 Right units (fig. 4–11).

11. Sew a Left Fabric 3 unit to a Right Fabric 4 unit. Press seam open. Make fifty-six (56) Fabric 3/Fabric 4 units (fig. 4–12). Unit should equal 4½" x 4½".

12. Sew a Left Fabric 4 unit to a Right Fabric 3 unit. Press seam open. Make fifty-six (56) Fabric 4/Fabric 3 units (fig. 4–13).

Quilt Construction

Follow the Quilt Layout illustration for the remainder of instructions (fig. 4–14, p. 40).

13. Layout the Block 1, 2, and 3 using the Quilt Layout illustration (fig. 4–14, p. 40), rotating blocks as shown.

14. Sew blocks together following general piecing instructions on pp. 25–27.

Fig. 4–8

Fabric 4
Left unit

Fig. 4–9

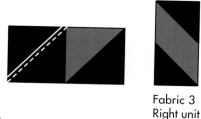

Fig. 4–10

Fabric 3
Right unit

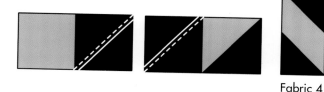

Fig. 4–11

Fabric 4
Right unit

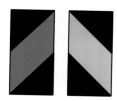

Fig. 4–12

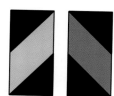

Fig. 4–13

Fig. 4–14. Quilt Layout

Tip

If your border section is too wide, sew some of the seams slightly bigger until you get the correct size. If it is too small, "unsew" and make some slightly smaller.

Border Construction

15. Sew the six (6) 3" x WOF Fabric 5 strip sets, short ends together. Press seams open. Trim to two (2) 3" x 51½". Match centers and ends, pin and sew to sides. Press to border.

16. Trim remaining 3" Fabric 5 strips to two (2) 3" x 56½". Match centers and ends, pin and sew to top and bottom. Press to border.

17. Sew fourteen (14) Fabric 4/Fabric 3 pieced units. Press to last unit sewn. Make two (2). Border section should equal 56½" long. Match the center and ends, pin and sew to the sides (fig. 4–15). (Pay attention to direction of the strips when piecing to quilt.) Press to border 1.

18. Sew fourteen (14) Fabric 3/Fabric 4 pieced units together. Press to last unit sewn on. Make two (2). Border section should equal 56½" long (fig. 4–16).

19. Make a corner unit by sewing a 2½" Fabric 5 square to a 2½" Fabric 3 square. Then, sew a 2½" x 4½" Fabric 5 rectangle to the top. Make two (2). Repeat with the 2½" Fabric 4 square for two (2) more corner units (fig. 4–17).

20. Sew a Fabric 4 corner unit to the right side and a Fabric 3 corner unit to the left side of the two remaining pieced border strips as shown (fig. 4–18). Matching center and ends, pin and sew to top and bottom. (Pay attention to direction of the strips when piecing to quilt.) Press to border 1.

21. Sew the seven (7) 1½" x WOF Fabric 5 strip sets, short ends together. Press seams open. Measure through the vertical center of the quilt, cut two (2) strips to this length. Match centers and ends, pin and sew to sides. Press to border 3.

22. Measure through the horizontal center of the quilt. Cut two (2) of remaining 1½" x WOF Fabric 5 strips to this width. Match centers and ends, pin and sew to top and bottom. Press to border 3.

23. Layer pieced backing, batting, and quilt top. Quilt as desired.

24. Follow the directions for sewing on the binding with the seven 2¼" Fabric 5 strips on pp. 79–80.

Fig. 4–15

Fig. 4–16

Fig. 4–17

Fig. 4–18

FUN HOUSE MIRRORS, 75" x 75", made and quilted by the author.

-- FUN HOUSE MIRRORS --

Quilt size: 75" x 75"
Block size: 14½"
Template size: 13"

For this quilt, I chose a symmetrical fabric that would create interesting mirror images. The fabric is from In The Beginning by Jason Yentor. See the chapter on using mirrors on pp. 16–17 and how to cut out the repeats to create a mirrored effect. Because of the way the fabrics look in the diamond, I tilted the block and framed it with black to accent the center star. Each star has a different repeat in the center but the outside patches are the same in each block.

Fabric Requirements *(substitute your own colors)*

Fabric 1: Symmetrical fabric – 2 to 2½ yards
Fabric 2: Green print – 1 yard
Fabric 3: Light Blue print – 1 yard
Fabric 4: Dark Blue print – ⅔ yard
Fabric 5: Black – 2¾ yards for blocks, sashing, and binding.
Fabric 6: Border stripe or large print – 2¼ yards
Backing: 4½ yards
Batting: 81" x 81"

Two (2) 12" x 18" sheets of heavy plastic template material.

Cutting Instructions

(Based on 40" WOF-Width of Fabric)

Fabric 1

* Cut sixteen (16) different sets of four (4) left and four (4) right identical repeats with Template A.

Fabric 2

* Cut seven (7) 4" x WOF strips; subcut into 128 C.

Fabric 3

* Cut seven (7) 4" x WOF strips; subcut into 128 C.

Fabric 4

* Cut four (4) 4½" x WOF strips; subcut into sixty-four (64) D.

Fabric 5

* Cut twenty-two (22) 2" x WOF strips; subcut into thirty-two (32) 2" x 13½" rectangles and thirty-two (32) 2" x 16½" rectangles.
* Cut six (6) 1½" x WOF strips; subcut into twelve (12) 1½" x 15" rectangles.
* Cut eleven (11) 1½" x WOF strips for sashing strips.
* Cut eight (8) 2¼" x WOF strips for the binding.

Fabric 6

(LOF refers to Length of Fabric)

* Cut four (4) 5½" x 81" length of fabric (LOF) along four (4) of the same border stripes or four (4) strips 5½" x 81" LOF if you use a large print.

Block Construction

Follow general piecing instructions for the block, pp. 25–27, making the following blocks:

Block

1.   Layout one set of four (4) left and four (4) right repeats from Fabric 1, eight (8) Fabric 2 C, eight (8) Fabric 3 C, and four (4) Fabric 4 D. Make sixteen (16) blocks (fig. 5–1).

2.   Tape the two large 12" x 18" sheets of template plastic together along the 18" edge. It will measure 24" x 36". Draw a 15" square on the templates with a permanent marker. Along the top measure ½" in from the left edge and mark it with a permanent marker. Measure 1⅝" in from the right edge and mark it with a permanent marker. Turn the template (drawn line side down) clockwise and repeat the above marking. Connect the ½" mark on the top left to the 1⅝" mark on the bottom left. Continue in this manner around the square. Cut out the 15" square with a pair of scissors (fig. 5–2, p. 45).

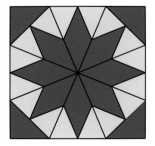

Fig. 5–1. Make 16.

3. Sew a 2" x 13½" strip along the left and right edges of the sixteen (16) blocks. Press to strip. Sew a 2" x 16½" strip along the top and bottom edges of the block. Press to strip (figs. 5–3a and 5–3b).

4. Place the template square on top of the block, lining up the inside block with the inside drawn square on the template (center it on the inside block if it doesn't quite match the inside lines). It will be tilted. Trim around template. Make eight (8). Turn template upside down and trim remaining eight (8) in the same manner (figs. 5–4a and 5–4b).

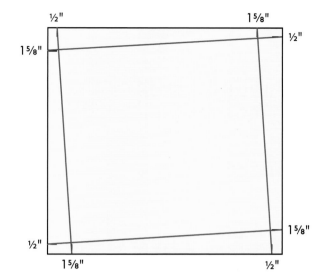

Fig. 5–2. 15" block

Fig. 5–3a

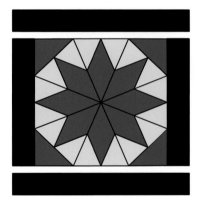

Fig. 5–3b

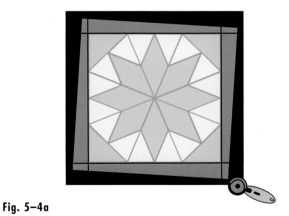

Fig. 5–4a

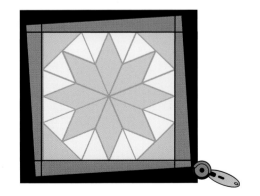

Fig. 5–4b

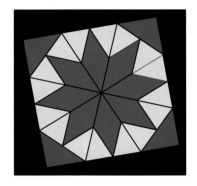

Fig. 5–5a

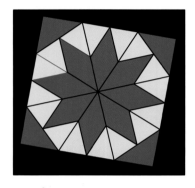

Fig. 5–5b

The resulting blocks will look like this (figs. 5–5a and 5–5b).

Quilt Top Assembly

Follow the Quilt Layout illustration (fig. 5–6, p. 47) for the following steps:

5. Sew 1½" x 15" sashing strips to four (4) blocks in each row. Press to sashing strips.

6. Sew the eleven (11) 1½" x WOF Fabric 5 strips together with diagonal seams. Trim to five (5) 1½" x 60½" (or your own personal measurement).

7. Sew the four (4) block rows together with the 1½" x 60½" strip sets as illustrated in the quilt layout.

8. Measure through the horizontal center of the quilt (side to side) and trim the remaining 1½" Fabric 5 strip to two (2) of these measurements. Sew to top and bottom.

Border Assembly

9. Follow the directions for mitering borders in the on p. 77 with the four (4) 5½" x 81" Fabric 6 border strips.

10. Layer pieced backing, batting, and quilt top. Quilt as desired.

11. Follow the directions for sewing on the binding with the eight (8) 2¼" Fabric 6 strips on pp. 79–80.

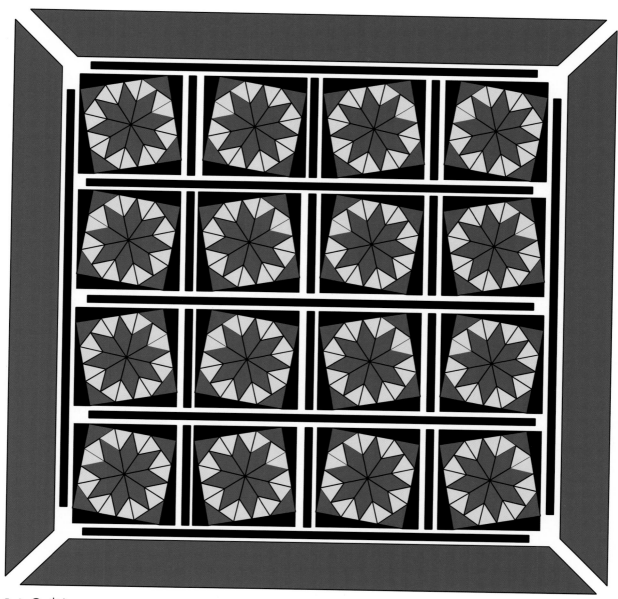

Fig. 5–6. Quilt Layout

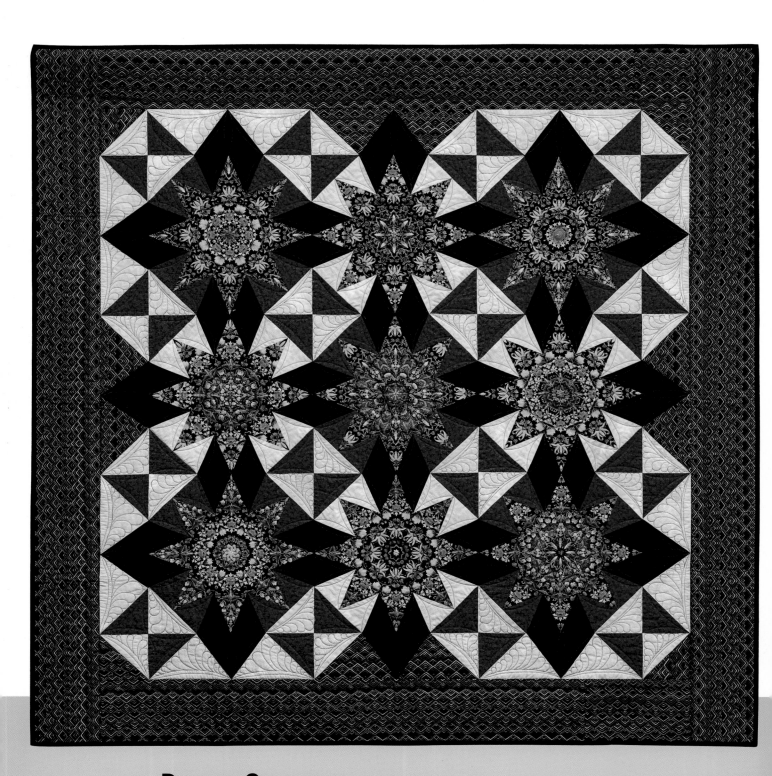

ROYAL GARDEN, 56¾" x 56¾", made by the author.
Quilted by Sandy Etheridge, Affton, Missouri.

❖❖ ROYAL GARDEN ❖❖

Quilt size: 56¾" x 56¾"
Block size: 13"
Border templates on p. 89

Sometimes a fabric collection just jumps out and grabs me. That is what happened when I saw this beautiful red/gold fabric collection, Eden, by Chong-a Hwang with Timeless Treasures. By cutting out all of the repeats in each block in the same area and sewing them together in the same direction, it created some wonderful kaleidoscope effects. I added the red and melon colored fabrics to accent those colors in the main print. The melon color really pops out of the star with those accent fabrics. I think the black fabric gives it a regal look.

This quilt has a pieced border, matching the edges of the block that make the straight set look like they are on point. You will need to make templates (p. 89) for this border. Since it is a pieced border, it is important that your blocks measure at 13½" unfinished so that the quilt edges match the finished border sections.

Fabric Requirements *(substitute your own colors)*

Fabric 1: Symmetrical fabric – 1½ to 2 yards
Fabric 2: Light – ⅞ yard
Fabric 3: Red – ½ yard
Fabric 4: Black – 1⅜ yard for blocks and binding
Fabric 5: Coordinating print – 1¾ yard for border
Backing: 3½ yards
Batting: 63" x 63"

Cutting Instructions

(Based on 40" WOF-Width of Fabric)

*HST refers to Half-square triangles. Squares cut once diagonally to create two (2) triangles.

Fabric 1

* Cut nine (9) different sets of eight (8) identical prints Template A.

Fabric 2

* Cut two (2) 4" x WOF strips; subcut into thirty-two (32) Template C.
* Cut two (2) 4½" x WOF strips; subcut into twenty (20) Template D.
* Cut two (2) 4½" squares; subcut once diagonally into four (4) 4½" *HST.
* Cut one (1) 4¼" x WOF strip. Fold fabric strip in half, wrong sides together, and make eight (8) cuts with Template F across the strip. You will have sixteen (16) total, eight (8) right and eight (8) left F sections. (Keep left and right pieces in separate labeled baggies.)
* Cut one (1) 4¼" x WOF strips. Fold fabric strip in half, wrong sides together, and make eight (8) cuts with Template G across the strip. You will have sixteen (16) total, eight (8) right and eight (8) left G sections. (Keep left and right pieces in separate labeled baggies.)

Fabric 3

* Cut one (1) 4" x WOF strips; subcut into twenty (20) Template C.
* Cut one (1) 4½" x WOF strips; subcut into sixteen (16) Template D.

* Cut one 4¼" x WOF strip. Fold fabric strip in half, wrong sides together, and make eight (8) cuts with Template G across the strip. You will have sixteen (16) total, eight (8) right and eight (8) left G sections. (Keep left and right pieces in separate labeled baggies.)

Fabric 4

* Cut four (4) 4" x WOF strips; subcut into seventy-two (72) Template C.
* Cut two (2) 4¼" x WOF strip. Fold fabric in half, wrong sides together. Make twelve (12) cuts with Template H across the strip. You will have twenty-four (24) total, twelve (12) left and twelve (12) right H sections. (Keep left and right pieces in separate labeled baggies.)
* Cut six 2¼" x WOF strips for the binding.

Fabric 5

(LOF refers to Length of Fabric)

* Cut border strips first.
* Cut two (2) 5½" x 48" strips LOF for border.
* Cut two (2) 5½" x 58" strips LOF for border.
* Cut one (1) 4¼" x 40" LOF strip. Fold fabric strip in half, wrong sides together, and make eight (8) cuts with Template F across the strip. You will cut sixteen (16) total, eight (8) right and eight (8) left F sections at the same time. (Keep left and right pieces in separate labeled baggies.)
* Cut two (2) 4½" squares; subcut once diagonally into four (4) 4½" *HST.

Block Construction

Block 1

1. Using the general piecing instructions, pp. 25–27, make four (4) blocks following the illustration. All A patches will go in the same direction.

Eight (8) Fabric 1 A, eight (8) Fabric 3 C, eight (8) Fabric 4 C, and four (4) Fabric 2 D (fig. 6–1).

Fig. 6–1. Block 1. Make 4.

Block 2

2. Using the general piecing instructions, pp. 25–27, make five (5) blocks following the illustration. All A patches will go in the same direction.

Eight (8) Fabric 1 A, eight (8) Fabric 2 C, eight (8) Fabric 4 C, and four (4) Fabric 3 D (fig. 6–2).

Fig. 6–2. Block 2. Make 5.

Pieced Border Construction

BORDER SECTION 1

3. Sew Fabric 3 Template G left, Fabric 2 Template F left, and Fabric 4 Template H left as illustrated. Press in the direction of the arrows. Make eight (8) left sections. Section should equal 4¼" x 6½" (fig. 6–3).

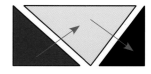

Fig. 6–3. Make 8.

4. Sew Fabric 3 Template G right, Fabric 2 Template F right, and Fabric 4 Template H right as illustrated. Press in direction of the arrows. Make eight (8) right sections (fig. 6–4).

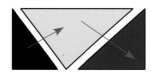

Fig. 6–4. Make 8.

BORDER SECTION 2

5. Repeat steps 3 and 4 with the Fabric 2 Template G left, Fabric 5 Template F left, and Fabric 4 Template H left and right sections. Press in the direction of the arrows. Make four (4) left (fig. 6–5) and four (4) right sections (fig. 6–6).

Fig. 6–5. Make 4.

Fig. 6–6. Make 4.

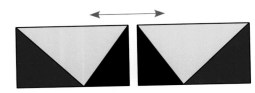

Fig. 6–7. Make 8.

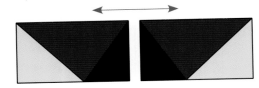

Fig. 6–8. Make 4.

Fig. 6–9. Make 4.

6. Sew a left Border Section 1 to a right Border Section 1. Press seam open. Make eight (8) Border section 1 (fig. 6–7).

7. Sew a left Border Section 2 to a right Border Section 2. Press seam open. Make four (4) border section 2 (fig. 6–8).

8. Sew a Border Section 1 to the left and right sides of a Border Section 2. Press seams open. Make four (4). Border should equal 39½" (fig. 6–9).

Quilt Construction

Follow the Quilt layout illustration (fig. 6–10, p. 53) for the following instructions.

9. Sew Blocks 1 and 2 in three across and three down. Press seams open.

10. Sew a pieced border to the left and right sides of the quilt top, matching centers, seams, and ends. Press to border units. Pay attention to the direction of the border section before pinning and sewing.

11. Sew a 4½" Fabric 2 HST to a 4½" Fabric 5 HST (fig. 6–11). Press to dark. Make four (4).

12. Sew the Fabric 2/Fabric 5 HST unit to each end of the two (2) remaining pieced borders. (See Quilt Layout illustration.) Press to border.

13. Matching centers, seams, and ends, sew these to the top and bottom. Pay attention to the direction of the border section before pinning and sewing.

Fig. 6–11

Border Construction

14. Measure through the vertical center of the quilt. Trim the two (2) 5½" x 48" Fabric 5 strips to this measurement. Match center and ends, pin and sew to sides. Press to border.

15. Measure through the horizontal center of the quilt. Trim the two (2) 5½" x 58" Fabric 5 strips to this measurement. Press to border.

Match center and ends, pin and sew to top and bottom.

16. Layer pieced backing, batting, and quilt top. Quilt as desired.

17. Follow the directions for sewing on the binding with the six 2¼" Fabric 6 strips on pp. 79–80.

Fig. 6–10. Quilt Layout

Using Two Fabrics

MARDI GRAS, 60½" x 60½", made by the author.
Quilted by Terri Kanyuck, Fenton, Missouri.

-- MARDI GRAS --

Quilt size: 60½" x 60½"
Block size: 17"

I really liked the jewel tones in Paula Nadelstern's most recent collection, Fabracadabra. There were so many different colors to pick from for the coordinating fabrics! Using two coordinating symmetrical fabrics that are close in color creates a subtle kaleidoscope effect. The further you step away from the quilt, the more it becomes apparent. The light background and dark connecting triangles are a stark contrast and create a wonderful movement across the quilt. The gold fabric brings out the gold tones in the center stars. They also frame the blocks and make an interesting star-like pattern where the blocks come together.

Sometimes when I am putting a quilt together I get a pleasant surprise. In the case of this quilt, it was the border. The curves of the print created a wonderful scallop-looking frame around the quilt and the small ¼" strip of gold adds a simple accent separating the striped border from the inside quilt. The layout is set on point so you will need to sew setting and corner blocks.

Fabric Requirements *(substitute your own colors)*

Fabric 1: Symmetrical fabric 1 – ½ yard
Fabric 2: Symmetrical fabric 2 – 1½ yard
Fabric 3: Light – 1½ yard
Fabric 4: Dark (fuchsia) – 1½ yard
Fabric 5: Bright (gold) – 1 yard
Fabric 6: Border stripe or large coordinating print
(Including binding) – 2 yards
Backing: 3¾ yards
Batting: 66" x 66"

Cutting Instructions

(Based on 40" WOF-Width of Fabric)

Fabric 1

* Cut five (5) different sets of four (4) identical prints with Template A. (Fabric 1 set 1)
* Cut four (4) different sets of two (2) identical prints with Template A. (Fabric 1 Set 2)
* Cut one (1) set of four (4) identical prints with Template A. (Fabric 1 Set 3)

Fabric 2

* Cut five (5) different sets of four (4) identical prints with Template A. (Fabric 2 set 1)
* Cut one set of four (4) identical prints with Template A. (Fabric 2 set 2)

Fabric 3

* Cut four (4) 4" x WOF strips; subcut into seventy-two (72) Template C.
* Cut one (1) 4½" x WOF strip; subcut into sixteen (16) Template D.

Fabric 4

* Cut four (4) 4" x WOF strips; subcut into sixty-four (64) Template C.
* Cut one (1) 4½" x WOF strip; subcut into sixteen (16) Template B.
* Cut six (6) 1½" x WOF strips.

Fabric 5

* Cut eight (8) Template D
* Cut sixteen (16) Template E.
* Cut six (6) ¾" x WOF strips.

Fabric 6

* Cut four (4) 5½" x 66½" x LOF strips.
* Cut four (4) 2½" x 66½" x LOF strips for binding.

Block Construction

Block 1

1. Using the general piecing instructions, pp. 25–27, make four (4) blocks following the illustration. Alternating in the diamond.

Four (4) identical Fabric 1 A, four (4) identical Fabric 2 A, eight (8) Fabric 3 C, eight (8) Fabric 4 C, and four (4) Fabric 3 D (fig.7–1, p. 57).

Block 2

2. Using the general piecing instructions, pp. 25–27, make one (1) block following the illustration. The block uses four (4) Fabric 1 Set 1 A, and four (4) Fabric 2 Set 1 A, alternating in the diamond.

Four (4) identical Fabric 1 A, four (4) identical Fabric 2 A alternating in the diamond, eight (8) Fabric 3 C, eight (8) Fabric 4 C, and four (4) Fabric 5 D (fig.7–2, p. 57).

Setting Block

3. Using the general piecing instructions for the setting block, pp. 26–27, make four (4) setting triangles following the illustration.

Two (2) identical Fabric 1 A Set 2, and one (1) Fabric 2 Set 2 A in the center diamond, four (4) Fabric 3 C, four (4) fabric 4 C, one (1) Fabric 5 D, and two (2) Fabric 5 E (fig. 7–3).

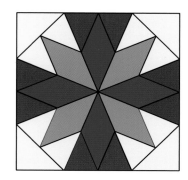

Fig. 7–1. Block 1. Make 4.

Corner Block

4. Using the general piecing instructions for the corner block, p. 27, make four (4) corner units following the illustration. This block uses the remaining four (4) Fabric 1 Set 3 A, two (2) Fabric 3 C, two (2) Fabric 4 C, two (2) Fabric 4 B, and two (2) Fabric 5 E (fig. 7–4).

Fig. 7–2. Block 2. Make 1.

Quilt Construction

5. Layout the blocks, setting triangles, and corner units using the Quilt Layout illustration (fig. 7–5, p. 58).

6. Following the general piecing instructions on pp. 25–27, piece the blocks together with the corner triangles and setting triangles.

Fig. 7–3. Setting triangle. Make 4.

Border Construction

7. Sew the six (6) 1½" x WOF Fabric 4 strip sets, short ends together. Press seams open. Measure through the vertical center of the quilt. Cut two (2) strips to this length. Match centers and ends, pin and sew to sides.

8. Measure through the horizontal center of the quilt. Cut two (2) of the remaining 1½" Fabric 4 strip to this width. Match centers and ends, pin and sew to top and bottom.

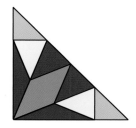

Fig. 7–4. Corner block 1. Make 4.

9. Sew the ¾" x WOF Fabric 5 strips, short ends together. Press seams open. Trim four to (4) ¾" x 54".

Tip

To get that perfect ¼" border with Fabric 5, use the edge of a ¼" foot lined up with the previous stitching line when sewing.

10. Matching centers, pin and sew the four (4) ¾" Fabric 5 strips to the four (4) 5½" Fabric 6 strips. (***Do not sew strips together without pinning.***)

11. Follow mitering instructions on p. 77 to sew the four (4) Fabric 5/Fabric 6 border strips to the quilt.

12. Layer pieced backing, batting, and quilt top. Quilt as desired.

13. Follow the directions for sewing on the binding with the four (4) 2¼" x 66½" Fabric 6 strips on pp. 79–80.

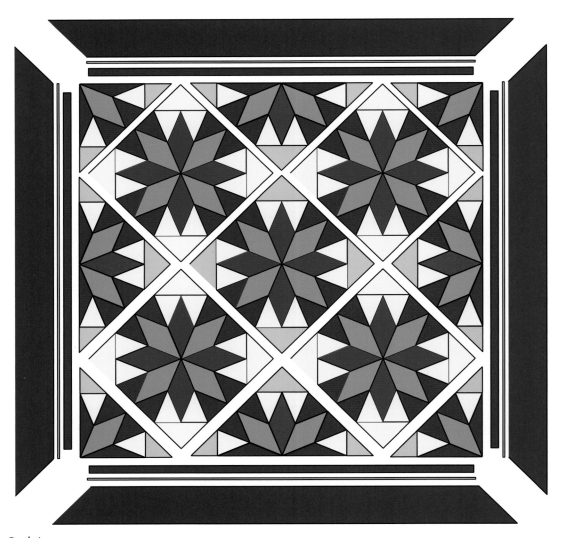

Fig. 7–5. Quilt Layout

CARIBBEAN BLUES, 61" x 75", made by the author.
Quilted by Terri Kanyuck, Fenton, Missouri.

-- CARIBBEAN BLUES --

Quilt size: 61" x 75"
Block size: 13"

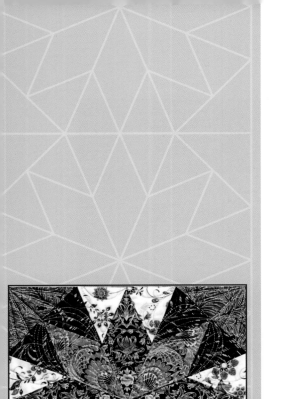

This quilt uses one symmetrical print and one repeating print in coordinating colors. Choose tone-on-tones for the dark, medium dark, and bright fabrics. The background light fabric can be a small print or a tone-on-tone.

Using sashing strips in a quilt can create some interesting effects. In the case of this quilt, the sashing is the same fabric as the background of the blocks, creating a floating effect. The dark corners in the blocks result in a flowing design across the quilt. The interplay of the light and dark blocks create an interesting pattern. The sign of a good quilt design is one that makes your eyes travel over the entire quilt.

Fabric Requirements *(substitute your own colors)*

Fabric 1: Symmetrical print – 1 to 1½ yards
Fabric 2: Coordinating print for fussy-cutting – 1 to 1½ yards
Fabric 3: Dark (black) – 1⅜ yards
Fabric 4: Medium dark (purple) – 1 yard
Fabric 5: Bright (turquoise for border 1 blocks) – ½ yard
Fabric 6: Light (blocks and border 1 blocks) – 2 yards
Fabric 7: Large print for the second border – 1⅜ yards
Backing: 3¾ yards
Batting: 67" x 81"

Cutting Instructions

(Based on 40" WOF-Width of Fabric)

Fabric 1

* Cut twelve (12) different sets of four (4) identical repeats with Template A.

Fabric 2

* Cut twelve (12) different sets of four (4) identical repeats with Template A.

Fabric 3

* Cut three (3) 4" x WOF strips; subcut into forty-eight (48) C triangles.
* Cut three (3) 4½" x WOF strips; subcut into thirty-six (36) D triangles.
* Cut four (4) 4½" x WOF strips; subcut into twenty-eight (28) 4½" x 4½" squares.

Fabric 4

* Cut three (3) 4½" x WOF strips; subcut into thirty-six (36) D triangles.
* Cut seven (7) 2¼" x WOF strips for the binding.

Fabric 5

* Cut five (5) 2½" x WOF strips; subcut into fourteen (14) 2½" x 1½" rectangles.
* Cut four (4) 4½" x 4½" squares.

Fabric 6

* Cut eight (8) 4" x WOF strips; subcut into 144 C triangles.
* Cut seven (7) 1½" x WOF strips; subcut into sixteen (16) 1½" x 13½" rectangles and eight (8) 1½" x 4½" rectangles.
* Cut seven (7) 1½" x WOF strips for long sashing strips.

* Cut five (5) 2½" x WOF strips; subcut into fourteen (14) 2½" x 13½" rectangles.

Fabric 7

* Cut seven (7) 5¾" x WOF strips for border.

Block Construction

Follow general piecing instructions, pp. 25–27, for the block making the following blocks:

Block 1

1. Layout one (1) set of four (4) like repeats from Fabric 1, one (1) set of four (4) like repeats from the Fabric 2, eight (8) Fabric 3 B, eight (8) Fabric 6 B, and four (4) Fabric 4 D. Make six (6) Block 1 (fig. 8–1).

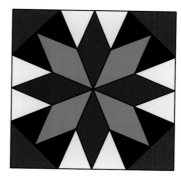

Fig. 8–1. Block 1. Make 6.

Block 2

2. Layout one (1) set of four (4) like repeats from the symmetrical fabric, one (1) set of four (4) like repeats from the medium print, sixteen (16) Fabric 6 C, and four (4) Fabric 3 D. Make six (6) Block 2 (fig. 8–2, p. 62).

Fig. 8-2. Block 2. Make 6.

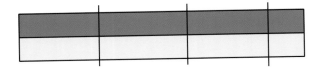

Fig. 8-3

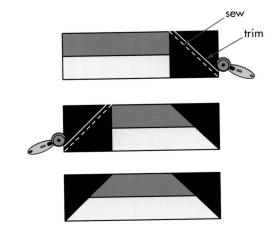

Fig. 8-4

Block 3

3. Sew a strip sets with the 2½" x WOF Fabric 6 and 2½" x WOF Fabric 5. Press to Fabric 6. Subcut into fourteen (14) 4½" x 13½" rectangles (fig. 8–3).

4. Draw a diagonal line on the backs of the twenty-eight (28) 4½" Fabric 3 squares. Place a 4½" Fabric 3 square, right sides together, on each end of the 4½" x 13½" Fabric 6/Fabric 5 pieced rectangle. Arranging the diagonal lines on the backs of the squares as illustrated. Sew along the diagonal lines, trim seams to ¼" and press to the triangle. Make fourteen (14) (fig. 8–4).

Quilt Construction

Follow the Quilt Layout illustration (fig. 8–5, p. 63) for the remaining instructions.

6. **Rows 1 and 6**—Sew a 4½" Fabric 5 square, alternate four (4) 1½" x 4½" Fabric 6 rectangles and three (3) Block 3 and end with a 4½" Fabric 5 square as in figure 8–5. Press to sash. Make two (2).

7. **Rows 2 and 4**—Sew the 1½" x 13½" fabric 6 sashing strips between two (2) Block 3, two (2) Block 1, and one (1) Block 2 as in figure 8–5. Press to sash. Make two (2).

8. **Rows 3 and 5**—Sew the 1½" x 13½" fabric 6 sashing strips between two (2) Block 3, two (2) Block 2, and one (1) Block 1 as in figure 8–5. Press to sash. Make two (2).

9. Sew the seven (7) 1½" x WOF Fabric

6 strips together. Trim to five (5) 1½" x 51½" strips. (Or your own personal measurement.)

10. Sew between each of the rows. Press to sash.

Border Construction

11. Sew the seven (7) 5¾" x WOF Fabric 7 strips, short ends together, with diagonal seams. Press seams open.

12. Follow the directions for sewing on the borders in the on p. 75 with the 5¾" Fabric 6 border strips.

13. Layer pieced backing, batting, and quilt top. Quilt as desired.

14. Follow the directions for sewing on the binding with the eight (8) 2¼" Fabric 4 strips on pp. 79–80.

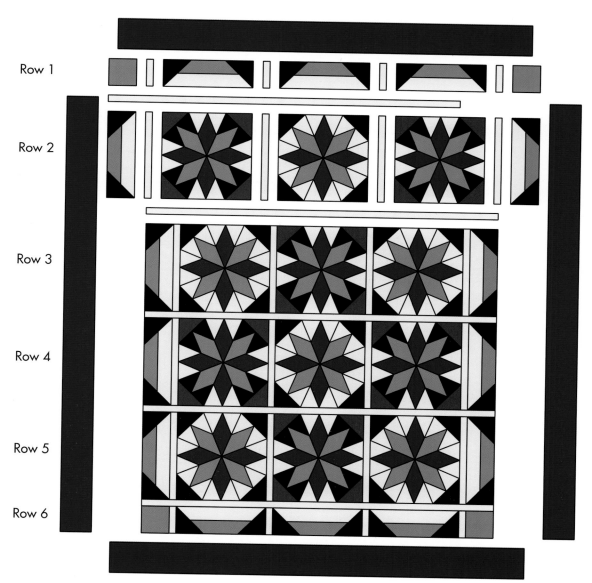

Row 1

Row 2

Row 3

Row 4

Row 5

Row 6

Fig. 8–5. Quilt Layout

CARNIVAL, 37" x 37", made and quilted by the author.

CARNIVAL

Quilt size: 37" x 37"
Block size: 13"

For this quilt, I chose two identical symmetrical fabrics with contrasting backgrounds from the same collection. The fabric is from Jinny Beyer's Carnival collection with RJR Fabrics. I cut the exact same repeat from the cream background and the black background. Sewing them together creates a continuous motif around the center of the block. Before attempting this type of quilt, you should check with both fabrics to see if they are exactly alike. If they are not it will be difficult to match the edges. The two-color background in the blocks, create an striking effect. The border fabric requires special cutting so that the design in the fabrics match at the mitered corner. Instructions are on p. 77. When using a border stripe with a large and small stripe, I like to use the smaller stripe for my binding to save fabric.

Fabric Requirements (substitute your own colors)

Fabric 1: Symmetrical light fabric – ½ to ¾ yard
Fabric 2: Identical symmetrical dark fabric – ½ to ¾ yard
Fabric 3: Light fabric – ½ yard
Fabric 4: Contrast fabric (gold) – ⅔ yard
Fabric 5: Bright fabric (fuchsia) – ¼ yard
Fabric 6: Border stripe or large print – 1¼ yard
Backing: 1¼ yard
Batting: 43" x 43"

Cutting Instructions

(Based on 40" WOF-Width of Fabric)

Fabric 1

* Cut four (4) different sets of four (4) identical repeats with Template A.

Fabric 2

* Cut four (4) different sets of four (4) identical repeats that match the light Fabric 1 repeats, with Template A.

Fabric 3

* Cut two (2) 4" x WOF strips; subcut into twenty-four (24) C triangles.
* Cut one (1) 4½" x WOF strip; subcut into four (4) D triangles.

Fabric 4

* Cut two (2) 4" x WOF strips; subcut into thirty-two (32) C triangles.
* Cut one (1) 4½" x WOF strip; subcut into twelve (12) D triangles.
* Cut four (4) 1½" x WOF strips.

Fabric 5

* Cut four (4) 1¼" x WOF strips.

Fabric 6

* Cut four (4) 4½" x 43" LOF stripes. (You may want to cut your strip longer in order to be able to place the center of the fabric motif in the center of the section so that the corners will match.) Choose one (1) of the wider border stripes if choosing a border stripe fabric.

Block Construction

Follow general piecing instructions, pp. 25–27, for the block making the following blocks:

Block

1. Layout two (2) sets of four (4) like light A repeats from Fabric 1, four (4) like dark A repeats *(matching Fabric 1 repeats)* from Fabric 2, six (6) Fabric 2 C, ten (10) Fabric 4 C, three (3) Fabric 4 D, and one (1) Fabric 3 D. Make four (4) (fig. 9–1).

Quilt Construction

Follow the Quilt Layout illustration for the remaining of the instructions (fig. 9–2, p. 67).

2. Sew the four (4) blocks together as in the Quilt Layout illustration rotating blocks as shown.

Border Construction

(Border strips are cut based on the correct measured size of the quilt. Your quilt measurement may be different, so be sure to measure your quilt top before cutting the strips.)

Fig. 9–1. Make 4.

3. Cut two (2) 1½" x WOF Fabric 4 strips to 1½" x 26½". Match centers and ends, pin and sew to sides.

4. Cut two (2) 1½" x WOF Fabric 4 strips to 1½" x 28½". Match centers and ends, pin and sew to top and bottom.

5. Repeat steps 3 and 4 with the 1¼" x WOF Fabric 5 strips.

6. Follow the directions for attaching the four (4) 4½" x 43" (or longer) Fabric 6 strips with mitered borders on p. 77.

7. Layer pieced backing, batting, and quilt top. Quilt as desired.

8. Follow the directions for sewing on the binding with the four (4) 2¼" x 43" Fabric 6 strips on pp. 79–80.

Fig. 9–2. Quilt Layout

Using Three Fabrics

NORTHERN LIGHTS, 50" x 50", made by the author.
Quilted by Ann McNew, Winfield, Missouri.

KALEIDOSTARS ✳ Toby Lischko

NORTHERN LIGHTS

Quilt size: 50" x 50"
Block size: 13"

I designed this quilt right after I made the quilt for Paula Nadelstern with her new Palindromes collection. In fact, this quilt is the one that inspired me to write this book. For your quilt, find three coordinating symmetrical fabrics. I chose a light one, and two contrasting fabrics. I like the contrast between the light and darker symmetrical fabrics and the ensuing design they create together. Using a dark and light symmetrical fabric accent the separate designs each one creates. The coordinating dark prints create both a frame around the blocks and a connecting movement across the blocks. Setting the blocks on-point makes a more interesting design with the partial setting and corner blocks.

Fabric Requirements

(yardage for symmetrical fabrics is an estimate)

Fabric 1: Symmetrical 1 – 1 to 1¼ yard
Fabric 2: Symmetrical 2 (light) – 1 yard
Fabric 3: Symmetrical 3 – ¾ yard
Fabric 4: Light – ⅞ yard for blocks and border 2
Fabric 5: Dark 1 – 1⅜ yards for blocks, border 1, and binding
Fabric 6: Dark 2 – 1½ yard for blocks and border 3
Backing: 3¼ yards
Batting: 56" x 56"

Cutting Instructions

(Based on 40" WOF-Width of Fabric)

Fabric 1: (Sym 1)

* Cut five (5) different sets of four (4) similar repeats each (for blocks) and four (4) different sets of two (2) similar repeats, for the setting triangles, with Template A.

Fabric 2: (Light Sym 2)

* Cut five (5) different sets of four (4) similar repeats with Template A. One (1) set will be used in the corner blocks.

Fabric 3: (Sym 3)

* Cut two (2) different sets of four (4) similar repeats with Template A. One (1) of the sets will be used in the setting triangles.

Fabric 4: (Light)

* Cut two (2) 4" x WOF strips; subcut into thirty-two (32) Template C.
* Cut one (1) 3⅜" x WOF strip; subcut into sixteen (16) Template E.
* Cut one (1) 4½" x WOF strips; subcut into eight (8) Template D.
* Cut five (5) 1½" x WOF for border 2.

Fabric 5: (Dark 1)

* Cut two (2) 4" x WOF strips; subcut into thirty-two (32) Template C.
* Cut one (1) 4½" x WOF strip; subcut into sixteen (16) Template D.

* Cut two (2) 2" x WOF strips; subcut sixteen (16) Template B.
* Cut five (5) 1½" x WOF for border 1.
* Cut six (6) 2¼" x WOF for binding.

Fabric 6: (Dark 2)

* Cut four (4) 4" x WOF strips; subcut into sixty-four (64) Template C.
* Cut six (6) 5" x WOF for border 3.

Block Construction

Follow general piecing instructions, pp. 25-27, for the block making the following blocks, setting triangles, and corner blocks:

Block 1

1. Layout one (1) set of four (4) like Template A repeats from Fabric 1, one (1) set of four (4) like Template A repeats from Fabric 2, eight (8) Fabric 6 C, eight (8) Fabric 5 C, and four (4) Fabric 5 D. Make four (4) blocks (fig. 10–1).

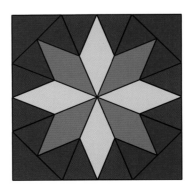

Fig. 10–1. Block 1. Make 4.

Block 2

2. Layout one (1) set of four (4) like Fabric 1 Template A repeats, one (1) set of four (4) like Fabric 3 Template A repeats, eight (8) Fabric 4 C, eight (8) Fabric 6 C, and four (4) Fabric 4 D. Make one (1) block (fig. 10–2).

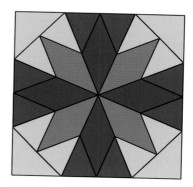

Fig. 10–2. Block 2. Make 1.

Setting Block

3. Layout one (1) set of two (2) like Fabric 1 repeats Template A, one (1) Fabric 3 repeat from second set Template A, four (4) Fabric 4 C, four (4) Fabric 6 C, one (1) Fabric 4 D, two (2) Fabric 4 E, and two (2) Fabric 5 B. Make four (4) (fig. 10–3).

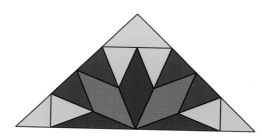

Fig. 10–3. Setting block. Make 4.

Corner Block

4. Layout one (1) Fabric 2 repeat from the remaining set of four (4) A, two (2) Fabric 4 C, two (2) Fabric 6 C, two (2) fabric 4 E, and two (2) Fabric 5 B (fig. 10–4).

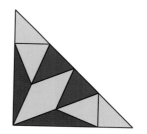

Fig. 10–4. Corner block. Make 4.

Quilt Construction

Follow the Quilt Layout illustration (fig. 10–5, p. 72) for the remaining of the instructions.

5. Layout the four (4) Block 1, one (1) Block 2, four (4) setting triangles, and four (4) corner blocks as illustrated. Construct top by following general setting instructions on pp. 25–27.

Border Construction

(Border strips are cut based on the correct measured size of the quilt. Your quilt measurement may be different, so be sure to measure your quilt top before cutting the strips.)

6. Follow basic border instructions on p. 75 for sewing on (in the following order) the 1½" Fabric 5 strips, 1½" Fabric 4 strips, and 5" Fabric 6 strips.

7. Layer pieced backing, batting, and quilt top. Quilt as desired.

8. Follow the directions for sewing on the binding with the six (6) 2¼" x WOF" Fabric 5 strips on pp. 79–80.

Fig. 10–5. Quilt Layout

-- FINISHING TECHNIQUES --

Basic layout, border construction, and binding techniques

Basic Layouts

For variety, I have chosen different quilt layouts in this book from straight sets, on-point sets, and sashing sets. With the Kaleidostar block, it adapts to any type of setting.

Straight set layouts CARNIVAL (fig. 11–1) quilt p. 64, ELECTRIFYING (fig. 11–2) quilt p. 35, and ROYAL GARDEN (fig. 11–3) quilt p.48

When sewing straight sets, without sashing strips, sew rows across first, press all seams open. Pressing the seams open where the blocks come together creates less bulk between where the star points come together. Then sew the rows together. Press these row seams open.

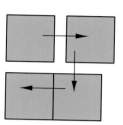

Fig. 11–1. CARNIVAL setting

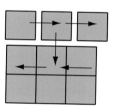

Fig. 11–2. ELECTRIFYING! setting

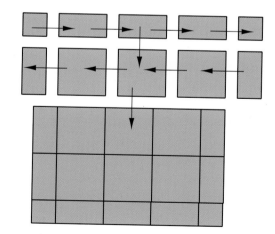

Fig. 11–3. ROYAL GARDEN setting

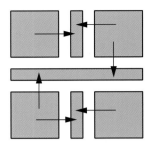

Fig. 11–4. Parfait setting

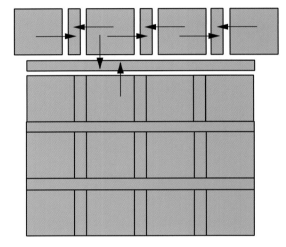

Fig. 11–5. Fun House Mirrors setting

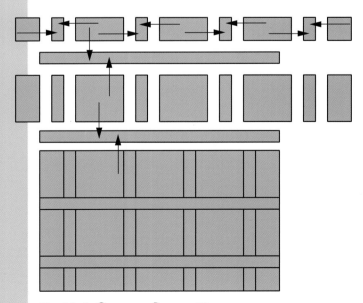

Fig. 11–6. Caribbean Blues setting

Straight set layouts with sashing

Parfait (fig. 11–4) quilt p. 30, Fun House Mirrors (fig. 11–5) quilt p. 42, and Caribbean Blues (fig. 11–6) quilt p. 59.

When sewing straight sets with sashing strips, treat the sashing strips and cornerstones (pieced or unpieced) as a row and always press towards the sashing strips.

On-Point Layouts

Mardi Gras (fig. 11–7) quilt p. 54 and Northern Lights (fig. 11–7) quilt p. 68.

When sewing on-point layouts, sew in diagonal rows with blocks and setting triangles. Press seams open. Sew row together. Press seams open. Sew corners on last.

Border Treatments

Sometimes thinking about what kind of border to put on a quilt is the hardest part of the design process. Do I do a pieced border, mitered border, or corner treatment? How many strips do I need in the border? How wide should I make it? I once read that the total border measurement should be about ¼ to ½ the width of a block. I sometimes start there, but usually I just do what is pleasing to my eye. If I have a border stripe, I will usually do a mitered corner, but there is no hard or fast rule. I always tell my students, "Do what makes it look right to you."

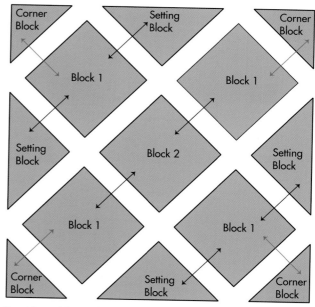

Fig. 11–7. Mardi Gras and Northern Lights setting

Basic Border Construction

The most efficient way to piece the borders is to piece all of the border strips at one time and then cut what you need for each side from the long strip. I find this method better than piecing each side separately because it usually uses less total strips. Sew all the same width border strips together with a diagonal seam (fig. 11–8). Use a smaller stitch when sewing and press these seams open. If the fabric pattern has a stripe or directional pattern, I will use a straight seam and match the stripes.

It is **very** important to measure the quilt before sewing the borders on. This will prevent those "wavy" borders. Before I measure for the borders, I will fold the top and bottom of the quilt top to meet in the middle of the quilt. They should be the same width as the center of the quilt. If they are I will take the middle measurement and

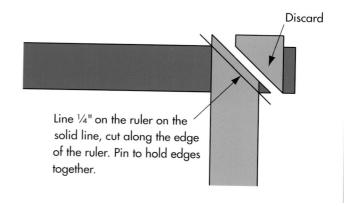

Discard

Line ¼" on the ruler on the solid line, cut along the edge of the ruler. Pin to hold edges together.

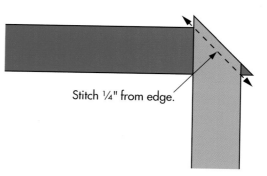

Stitch ¼" from edge.

Fig. 11–8. Sewing border strips

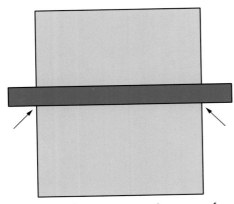

Lay border strips across the center of the quilt and clip at edges of the quilt top on both sides and trim, or measure through the center and cut border strips to this length.

Fig. 11–9

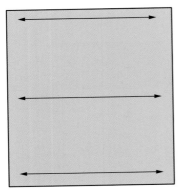

Take 3 measurements, if the quilt sides are not equal, add them together and divide by 3 for the average.

Fig. 11–10

trim my border strips to this width (fig. 11–9). If they are off more than ½" to 1", then I will take three measurements; top, middle, and bottom, add them together, and divide by 3. This will give me an average measurement to cut the strips at (fig. 11–10). Repeat this process with the length of the quilt top if it is not square. If it is a large quilt, lay the quilt on the floor or a bed and place the border strips across the quilt. Then mark or clip the strips at the edges of the quilt. Then take the border strips to your cutting table and use a rotary cutter and ruler to cut a straight edge at the clip.

When sewing on the borders it is important to match the centers and ends of the strips and the quilt and pin, pin, pin. To match the centers, fold the border with wrong sides together and the quilt right sides together to create a crease at the center of both. The two creases will fit into each other and make it easier to match and pin the center points. Pin each end and ease the remainder of the quilt or border, pinning frequently. It pins together better if you lay the quilt on a flat surface. If there is one side that seems to have a little more easing to it (which will happen if the sides are not equal), place it on the bottom towards the sewing machine when sewing. The feed dogs on the machine will help ease the excess fabric. If the quilt is large, also match the quarter points. Repeat this process for as many borders that you have.

For pieced borders, the accuracy of your blocks is important because you are sewing a border to a specific size. CARIBBEAN BLUES quilt, p. 59, and ELECTRIFYING, p. 35, have pieced borders. You should still measure through the center of the quilt and if you do have to make any adjustments to the border, make them at both ends, cutting equal amounts off each side.

For mitered borders it is important to cut enough extra fabric to allow for the mitered corner. Use the following rule of thumb: Take the border width measurement times two (2) and add an extra 6", then add that to the quilt measurement. For example: Finished border size is 5", 5 x 2 = 10 + 6 = 16. Therefore you will cut a border strip that is the width or length of the quilt plus 16".

When sewing on the mitered borders, you still need to mark the width of the quilt on the strips with pins. Fold the border strip and quilt in half and place a pin on the middle in each one.

Measure from the center of the quilt to the ends. Use this measurement from the center of the border strip and place a pin on each end. These pins will be used to match the quilt edges. Mark ¼" in from the edge of the quilt on the back of the corners and then sew with the border strip on the bottom towards the sewing machine. This way you can see where to start and stop stitching and backstitch at the ¼" mark (fig. 11–11). Sew on all four borders before mitering the corners. Press towards border.

For a perfect mitered corner, turn the quilt face up. Lay the border strip on the top of the quilt straight to the right. Take the right border strip, fold the end of the strip, starting at the ¼" seam intersection, under to create a 45° angle. The two border strips will be right sides together

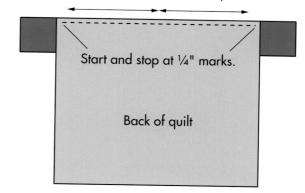

Measure from center and mark ends on border strips.

Start and stop at ¼" marks.

Back of quilt

Fig. 11–11

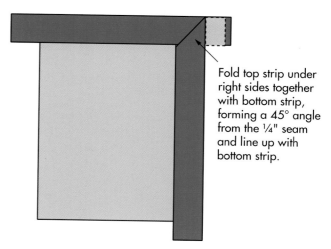

Fig. 11–12

Fold top strip under right sides together with bottom strip, forming a 45° angle from the ¼" seam and line up with bottom strip.

Tip

For the CARNIVAL quilt, the border strips have symmetry so I want the corners to match. To do this find the center of the design (it will be the same on both halves of the strip). Match the centers of the quilt and border, and follow the remainder of the directions.

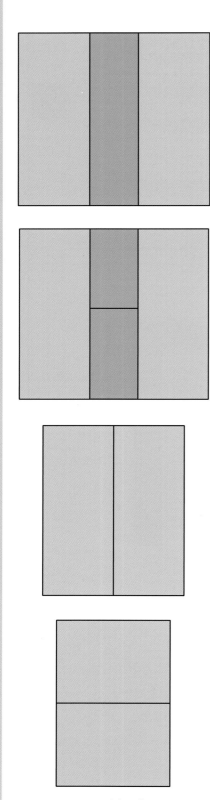

Fig. 11–13. Pieced backing options

and directly on top of one another. Take a square ruler with a 45° line and place it on the corner to check the "squareness" of it. The angle on the border miter should be at the 45° mark on the ruler and the corner should be square along the top edge of the ruler.

Make any adjustments at this time, with the top border strip, until it is completely square. Then place a couple of pins at the fold to hold the strips together and press it with an iron to make a sharp crease. Very carefully take out the pins and fold the quilt in half diagonally right sides together, being careful to keep the borders together (place a couple more pins to hold them right sides together). If you have trouble seeing the crease, use a marking instrument, to draw in the crease with a ruler.

Pin the borders along the line and sew, back stitching from the ¼" inside seam to the outside of the border strip along the marked line. Double check one last time by laying the corner flat to see if the corner is still square, using a square ruler and make any adjustment if necessary. Repeat with the other 3 borders. Trim the seams to ¼" and press the seams open (fig. 11–12, p. 77).

Pieced Backing

There are several options when piecing the backing (fig. 11–13). First, for large quilts, check with your longarm quilter, if you use one, to see if they prefer that the seams go horizontal or vertical to the quilt. They like the backs to be "squared up." It is just as important to piece the back as even as the front. They will also tell you how much larger they like the back, usually from 4" to 8" larger than the front.

Some quilts you can use two widths plus a smaller width in the center and others you will only need two pieces. You can save fabric by piecing the centerpiece.

Of course, don't discount using leftover scrap pieces on the back. Be sure when you piece them that the top and side edges are evenly trimmed.

Layering and Quilting

Layer the quilt top, batting, and backing. Baste using your favorite basting technique. If you have the quilt quilted by a longarm quilter, you do not need to baste the quilt. There are a variety of methods for basting. Spray basting is good for wall or smaller quilts. You can also use safety pins, tacking gun, or iron on batting. If you have a large quilt, get your quilting friends together and have a basting party at your favorite quilt shop if you do not have a table big enough to work on. It makes the job go much faster and is definitely more fun!

There are many ways to quilt these quilts. I find that quilting in-the-ditch (along the seam line) for the star helps make the blocks lay flat. I also do that between all of the border strips and blocks. If you have a very busy print or design you can try an all-over design. I feel the design of the quilt (the blocks and kaleidoscope effect) is the most important part and the quilting should accent it or just hold it together. I don't like my quilting to overpower my designs because I want people to focus on the stars.

After quilting, trim the backing and batting even with the edge of the quilt. Square off the corners with a large square ruler.

Binding

Sew binding strips together with diagonal seams using the same technique as described on p. 77 for piecing border strips. Fold binding strips lengthwise with wrong sides together and pin as you sew it to the quilt. I have found that pressing the binding strips in half with an iron is not all that necessary and is time saving. Match raw edges of binding to the front quilt edges starting about ⅓ down one side. It is a good idea to check, placing the binding around the edge of the quilt, to make sure that none of the seams end up on one of the corners. Using a ¼" seam, start sewing 8" from the end of the strip and stop ¼" before the corner (fig. 11–14, p. 80).

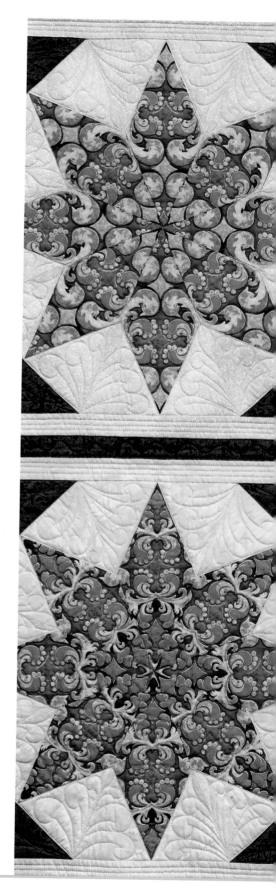

RIGHT: Parfait, quilting detail. Full quilt on p. 30.

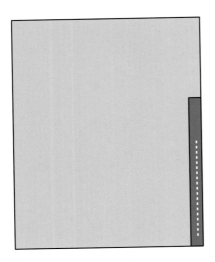

Fig. 11–14

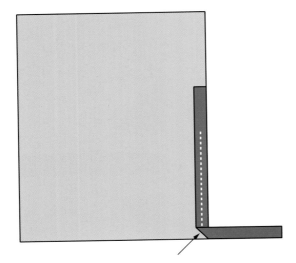

Fig. 11–15

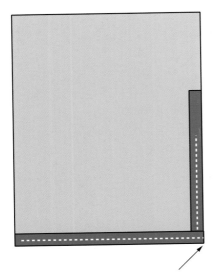

Fig. 11–16

Fold strip up forming a 45° angle. Fold down matching the fold to the edge of the quilt. Sew from the edge and to the next ¼" mark. Repeat the corner technique around the quilt (figs. 11–15 and 11–16).

Stop stitching 16" from the first stitching. Open the two strips (beginning and end), fold the end of the strip to meet the beginning of the other strip and crease. Measure 2¼" from crease and trim off the remainder. The two end pieces will overlap by 2¼". Match edges, right sides together, at a 90° angle like you did when you sewed the strips together; draw a diagonal line and stitch along the line. You will have to pull the strips out of the way of the quilt to do this. Trim to ¼". Press the seam open. Pin and continue sewing binding down.

Be sure to put a label on your quilt with your name, date and the name of anyone else who was involved with the making of it. You might also want to include if it was made for a special occasion and who it was made for.

Now for the most important part! Step back, take a look and admire your work. The finished quilt is always such an enjoyable experience for me. Usually it turns out much better than I expected. But most of all, the whole process for me was fun. Quilting should be fun, so enjoy your quilt and have fun making many more.

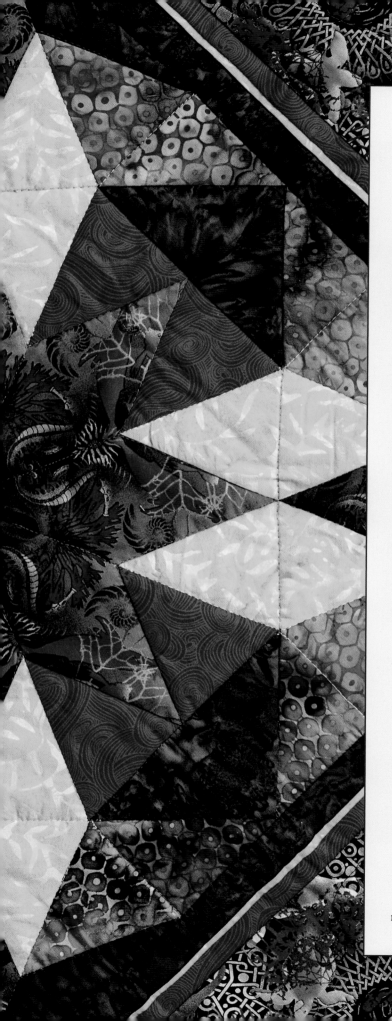

QUILT GALLERY

I have been teaching classes on my Kaleidostar block for a little over a year. Many of the quilters who have taken it have told me that this quilt is one they really want to finish! I told a couple of the groups that if they finished the quilt in time to be in my book to send them to me. These four quilts show how different one pattern can become by putting their own personal design elements into them. The first quilt in the gallery was done by a quilter who told me she only wanted to make one block and decided to do the "mirror" effect on it. She finished it in a couple weeks and sent me the image. I love how she created her own small quilt from the pattern! The other three quilts were slight variations of my Northern Lights pattern. It is amazing how different each one looks based on their fabric choices.

RIGHT: The Sea, detail. Full quilt on p. 82.

THE SEA, 27¼" x 27¼", made by Harriet Bain, Rolla, Missouri

MY FATHER'S MAJESTIC STAR, 49" x 49",
made by Brenda Barnhart, Rolla, Missouri

MANDARIN SUNSET, 47" x 47", made and quilted by
Janet Rankin, Belle, Missouri

KALEIDOSTARS * Toby Lischko

KALEIDOSCOPE STAR CASCADE, 50" x 50",
made and quilted by Diana Howard, Collinsville, Illinois.

TEMPLATES

The following six pages contain the templates for the 13" and 17" Kaleidostar blocks and the border treatment for ROYAL GARDEN. If you take them to the copy machine be sure to copy at full scale (100%) or no scaling. Measure the 1" square after copying to make sure it is to scale. Tape the images to the back of the template material and cut them out exactly on the outer line. Be sure to trim off the corners and trace the seam allowances and any other lines. If you prefer to purchase my acrylic templates for the 13" and 17" blocks (not the border treatment templates) they are available at: www.gatewayquiltsnstuff.com.

RIGHTT: CARNIVAL, detail. Full quilt on p. 64.

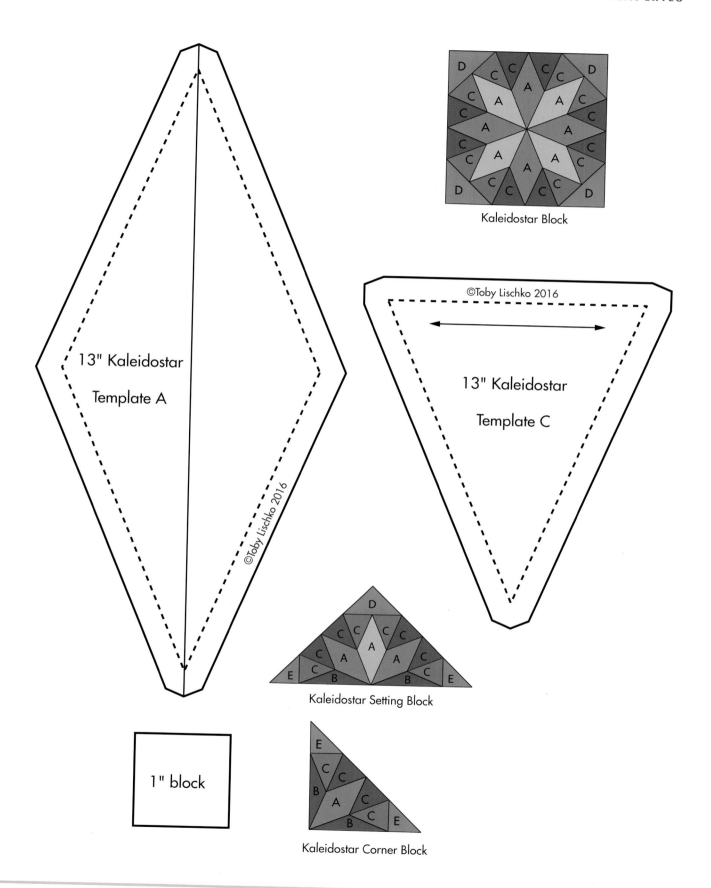

13" Kaleidostar

Template A

©Toby Lischko 2016

Kaleidostar Block

©Toby Lischko 2016

13" Kaleidostar

Template C

Kaleidostar Setting Block

1" block

Kaleidostar Corner Block

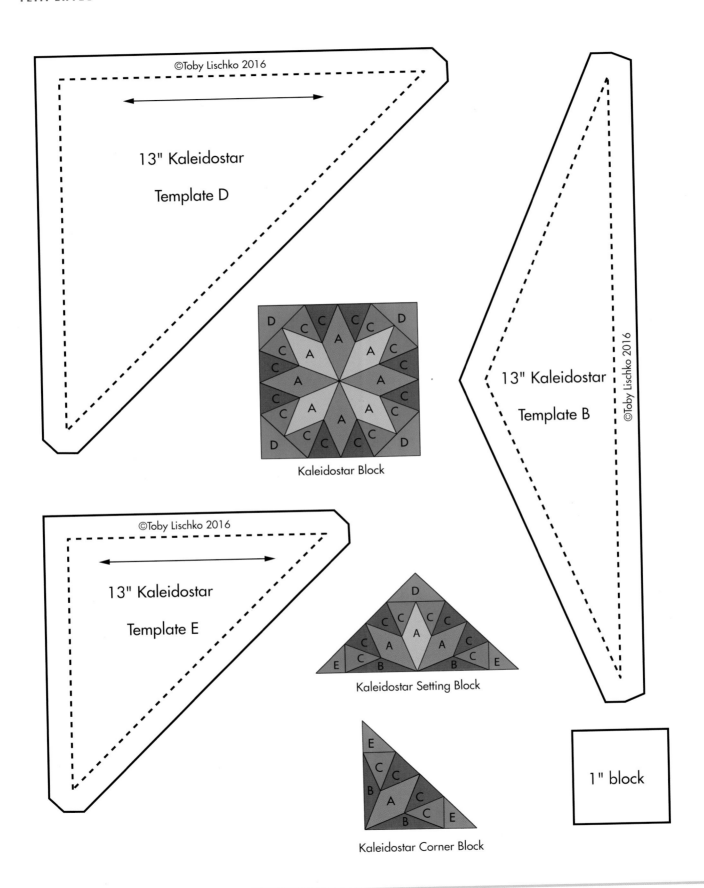

©Toby Lischko 2016

13" Kaleidostar

Template D

13" Kaleidostar

Template B

©Toby Lischko 2016

©Toby Lischko 2016

13" Kaleidostar

Template E

Kaleidostar Block

Kaleidostar Setting Block

Kaleidostar Corner Block

1" block

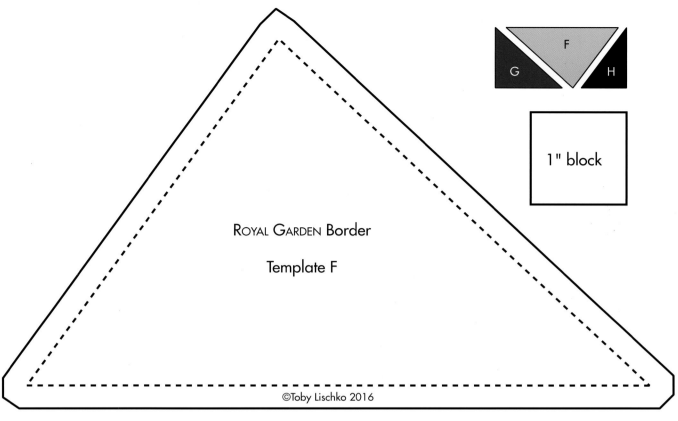

1" block

ROYAL GARDEN Border

Template F

©Toby Lischko 2016

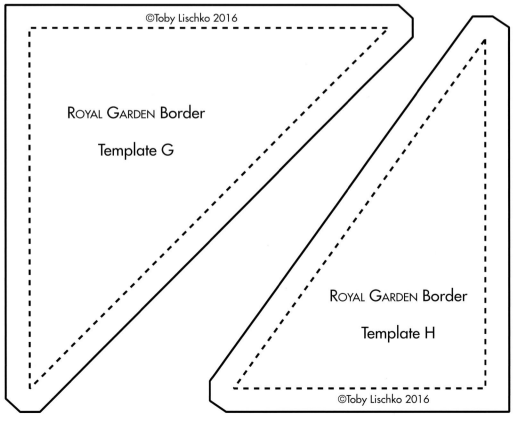

©Toby Lischko 2016

ROYAL GARDEN Border

Template G

ROYAL GARDEN Border

Template H

©Toby Lischko 2016

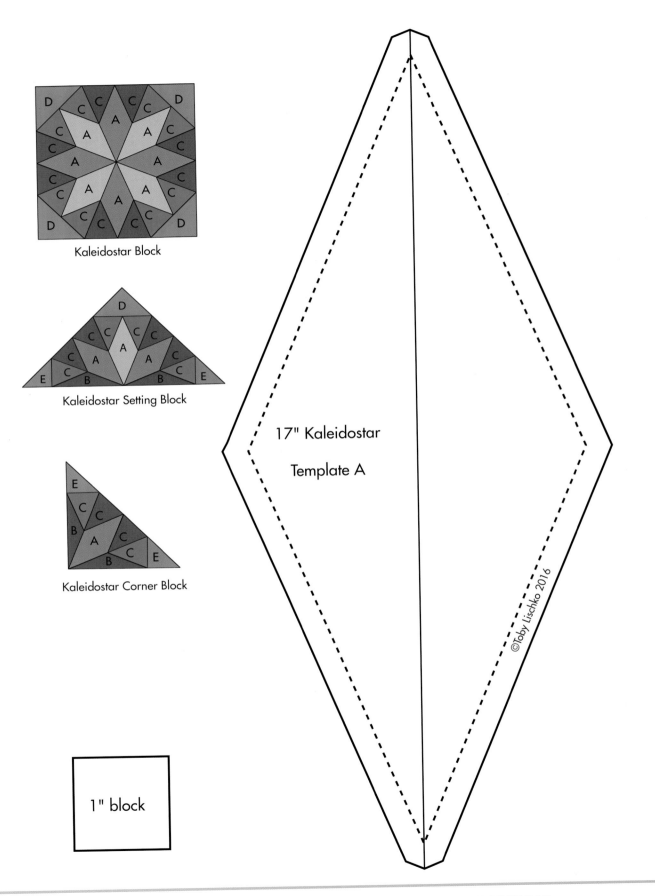

Kaleidostar Block

Kaleidostar Setting Block

Kaleidostar Corner Block

17" Kaleidostar

Template A

©Toby Lischko 2016

1" block

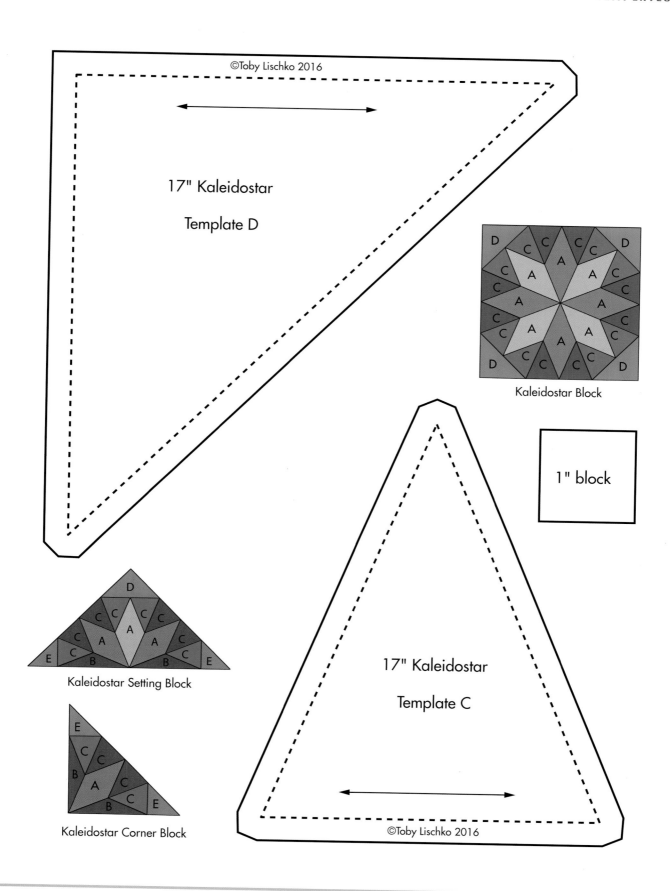

©Toby Lischko 2016

17" Kaleidostar

Template D

Kaleidostar Block

1" block

Kaleidostar Setting Block

Kaleidostar Corner Block

17" Kaleidostar

Template C

©Toby Lischko 2016

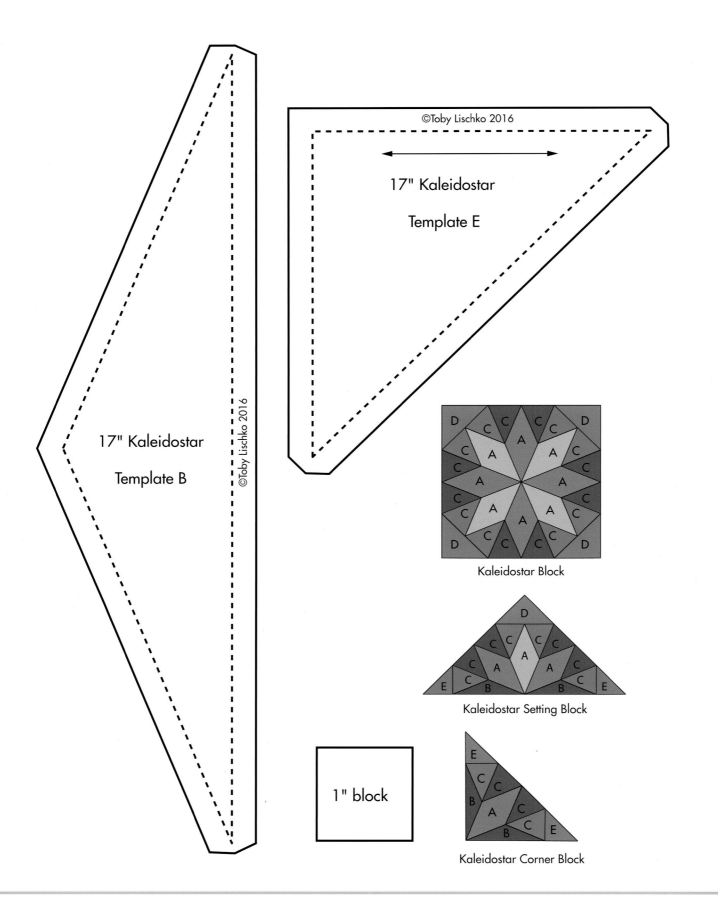

©Toby Lischko 2016

17" Kaleidostar

Template E

17" Kaleidostar

Template B

©Toby Lischko 2016

Kaleidostar Block

Kaleidostar Setting Block

1" block

Kaleidostar Corner Block

-◆- RESOURCES -◆-

I want to thank the following companies for their services and contributions to this book.

Brandy's Quilt Products, 1443 Hwy 84
Amity, AR 71921, www.brandysquiltpatterns.com

RJR Fabrics, 2610 Columbia Street, B
Torrance, CA 90503, www.rjrfabrics.com

Timeless Treasures, 483 Broadway
New York, NY 10013, www.ttfabrics.com

In The Beginning Fabrics, Seattle, Washington
www.inthebeginningfabrics.com

Benartex Fabrics, 132 West 36th Street, 4th Floor
New York, NY 10018, www.benartex.com

Electric Quilt, 419 Gould St., Suite 2
Bowling Green, OH, 43402, www.electricquilt.com

My company **Gateway Quilts & Stuff. Inc.**
212 Fox Meadow Lane, Beaufort, MO 63013
www.gatewayquiltsnstuff.com

You can order the template sets from my website or by contacting me through it.

LEFT: ELECTRIFYING!, detail. Full quilt on p. 35.

-- ABOUT THE AUTHOR --

PHOTO: Bryon Raterman

Toby was born to quilt! Her mother is a retired home economics teacher and her grandfather was a tailor. A crafter from an early age, who has tried every craft imaginable, from knitting, crocheting, tatting, needlepoint, cross stitch, English smocking, and macramé to name a few. Whatever craft was in vogue she tried. She started sewing her own clothes when she was 12. She even designed and sewed her own wedding gown. She enjoyed each of those crafts but eventually got bored and moved on to another.

Toby took her first quilting class in 1985, along with her mother, from the renowned quilter Jackie Robinson, who owned a local quilt shop in St. Louis, Missouri. It was during summer vacation from her job as a special education teacher and after the six-week class she got the quilting bug. In 1995 she started working in a quilt shop, began teaching quilting classes, and designing her own quilts. She was then asked to lecture and hold workshops with local quilt guilds. She also began to enter quilt contests. "I finally found a craft that was continually evolving and I was evolving with it. It is never boring!"

In 1998 she had her first quilt on the cover of *Miniature Quilt Magazine*, and won her first contest with the Hoffman Challenge, she was hooked! In 2001 she began to work with fabric companies and magazines, designing quilts and writing articles. In 2007, she retired from education and began concentrating on her quilting career, setting some high goals: to win a ribbon for a quilt in the American Quilter's Society Quiltweek®–Paducah, Kentucky; to teach at a national venue, and to write a book. In 2005 she won a first place prize in the First Entry, Wall division for her "masterpiece" CELESTIAL CROWNS, at the AQS Quiltweek®–

Paducah, which was also featured in the AQS 2006 calendar. She wrote her first book, *St. Louis Stars* in 2008. She has taught in many national quilt shows including IQA in Houston, Texas; AQS Quiltweek®–Paducah, Kentucky and Des Moines, Iowa; National Quilting Association, Original Sewing and Quilting Expo, and Machine Quilter's Expo.

An award winning quilter, pattern designer, author, and quilt teacher she enjoys the whole process. "I love taking a group of fabrics and creating a unique design that shows off the collection." Her skill and her unique style have been recognized by many of the major fabric companies, such as Timeless Treasures, Hoffman, Clothworks, Benartex, RJR, and P&B, who regularly commission her to design quilts for them.

Her teaching style is tempered from her years as a special education teacher, and her students have told her that she teaches to the quilters' styles, helping them understand even the most difficult techniques. They always come away from her workshops saying, "I didn't know I could do that!"

"I like to inspire quilters to go that one step beyond their everyday quilting and try something new. I don't think that there are any quilters who can not do what I do if they want to." She teaches techniques that students can use in any of their quilting projects. Her lectures and trunk shows give quilters ideas on how to approach their fabrics and blocks in non conventional ways. She

feels that there is an artist in everyone and they just need to find their niche, which is what she did when she started quilting. "Fabrics are my palette and the quilts are my paintings."

She considers herself a traditional quilter with a twist. "I use traditional blocks to create quilts that look difficult but that anyone can make." Her use of fabrics in the quilts can change the whole look of a traditional block. Her patterns and designs can be found in quilt shops, on the web, and in many of the national quilting magazines such as *McCall's Quilting*, *McCall's Quick Quilts*, *Fons and Porter*, *The Quilter*, *Quilter's Newsletter*, *Quiltmaker,* and *Quilt*. She was a featured artist in *Miniature Quilts* and wrote articles for *Quilter's World*.

She lives in the rural area of Beaufort, Missouri, with her husband Mike of 43 years, a Marine Corp, Vietnam Veteran, one dog and six cats. She runs her own business, Gateway Quilts & Stuff, Inc. and has a website www. gatewayquiltsnstuff.com where she sells her patterns and templates, and where her workshop descriptions can be found. She hopes that many readers, from beginners to accomplished quilters, will enjoy this book and find inspiration on every page.

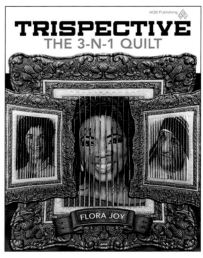

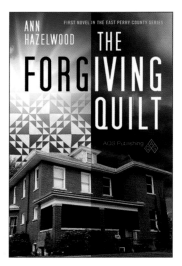
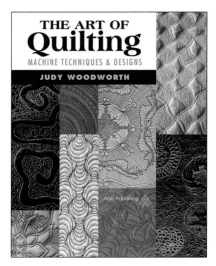

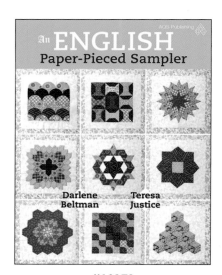